The Brilliant Cocktail Concept

Charles of the Ritz
& Carlos of Raffles

Bottle by Bottle you Build a Cocktail Bar

foulsham
LONDON • NEW YORK • TORONTO • SYDNEY

foulsham

The Oriel, Thames Valley Court, 183–187 Bath Road, Slough, Berkshire, SL1 4AA, England

Foulsham books can be found in all good bookshops and direct from www.foulsham.com

ISBN: 978-0-572-03597-6

Copyright © 2010 W. Foulsham & Co. Ltd

Cover photographs © Fresh Food Images

A CIP record for this book is available from the British Library

Contributing editor: Sue Parkin

Printed and bound by Scotprint, Haddington

INTRODUCTION

The Brilliant Cocktail Concept contains 365 cocktails, one for every day of the year. There are mouthwatering cocktails for all occasions: romantic cocktails to lure your lover on Valentine's Day, cool blue cocktails to sip by the pool on long summer days and warming punches for winter parties. Each cocktail is illustrated in full colour to give you an idea of what it looks like, which glass to serve it in and how to garnish it.

You can use **The Brilliant Cocktail Concept** as a cocktail maker's diary. Jot down your own comments on your cocktail making extravaganzas, your friends' birthdays, and to remind yourself of other occasions worth celebrating with a seasonal cocktail. Mark your own special occasions by making the cocktail for that day.

The book assumes that your drinks cupboard is empty at the start of the year. You can start adding drinks, one by one (47 drinks are added in total, at approximately weekly intervals), and at each stage have a large selection of cocktails to choose from. You'll gradually accumulate a good stock of drinks, and then the more complex cocktail ideas are suggested. Any cocktail given on a specific day will only contain the drinks that have been introduced by that date.

Preparing cocktails is simplified if ingredients, basic equipment and glasses are stored together. The location will obviously depend on space available: kitchen cupboards, a cocktail cabinet or shelves in a living room. Or, why not buy a trolley and prepare your cocktails in front of your guests?

YOUR COCKTAIL SHOPPING LIST

Gin	Week 1	Plymouth gin	Week 25
Italian vermouth	Week 2	Tequila	Week 26
Dubonnet	Week 3	Crème de banane	Week 27
French vermouth	Week 4	Maraschino/yellow Chartreuse	Week 30
Scotch whisky	Week 5	Kummel	Week 32
Pernod	Week 6	Amer Picon	Week 34
Brandy	Week 7	Benedictine	Week 35
Cointreau	Week 8	Sloe gin	Week 36
Green crème de menthe	Week 9	Fernet Branca	Week 37
Dry sherry	Week 10	Drambuie	Week 38
Green Chartreuse	Week 11	Irish whiskey	Week 39
Canadian club whisky	Week 12	Dark and golden rum	Week 40
White rum	Week 13	Kahlua	Week 41
Vodka	Week 14	Grand Marnier	Week 43
Campari	Week 15	Amaretto di Saronno	Week 44
Blue curaçao	Week 16	White crème de menthe	Week 46
Galliano	Week 17	Lillet	Week 47
Apricot brandy	Week 18	Crème de cacao	Week 48
Cherry brandy	Week 19	Tia Maria	Week 49
Swedish punsch	Week 20	Kirsch	Week 50
Calvados	Week 21	Ginger wine	Week 51
Orange or brown curaçao	Week 22	Demerara rum	Week 52
Crème de cassis/port	Week 23		

ABOUT THE COCKTAILS

How to find the cocktail you want to make

1 If you know the name of the cocktail, there is an alphabetical index on page 118.
2 If you want a particular kind of cocktail, e.g. a party cocktail, a non-alcoholic cocktail, an after-dinner cocktail or a nourishing nightcap, look at the lists on page 117 where you will find suggestions.
3 If you want a cheaper cocktail with fewer ingredients, look at the cocktails at the beginning of the book.
4 If you only have a couple of bottles in your drinks cabinet, look at the *Ingredients guide* on page 114, which will tell you which cocktails you can make with them.

Follow this book and you're going to have a great year!

Basic equipment needed

1 A shaker. This looks something like a miniature Thermos flask, and consists simply of two nickel containers that fit into each other.
2 A mixing glass. This is simply a large tumbler or bar glass.
3 A mixing spoon. This is like a teaspoon, holding about 5 ml, but with a long, thin handle.
4 A strainer.
5 A lemon squeezer.
6 A muddler. This is an implement used for crushing sugar or bruising fruit, mint, etc.
7 A millilitre measuring glass, graded with various fractional parts.

The above are the essentials. Of the other forms of equipment, many are part of the normal culinary equipment. Obviously a corkscrew and bottle opener are required, and for certain recipes a nutmeg grater will be needed. A fruit knife and a fork and spoon for handling fruit will be wanted, too, and there should be an ice pick and a scoop or tongs for handling ice. Finally, straws are needed for the longer drinks, and a bundle of cocktail sticks to allow simple manipulation of the cherries, olives, etc., that are served in certain cocktails.

Decanter bottles with stoppers are desirable for ingredients that have to be served in the small measurements known as dashes.

A few cocktails are best made in an electric blender.

Glasses

The photographs and recipes will give you a good guide to the ideal glass to use, but here is a list of the glasses available for serving drinks. Measurements are given as measures, and each measure is equal to 25 ml (5 tsp).

1 Cocktail glasses. Each holds about 75 ml (5 tbsp).
2 Small wine glasses or crusta glasses. Each holds about 110 ml (7 tbsp).
3 Wine glasses. Each holds about 150 ml (¼ pint).
4 Tumblers or highball glasses. Each holds about 300 ml (½ pint).
5 Sherbet glasses are like small tumblers.
6 Liqueur glasses. Each holds about 140 ml (scant ¼ pint). However, fine liqueurs are generally served in large balloon glasses. For ordinary purposes, a half-filled cocktail glass is suitable for the serving of liqueur.
7 Pousse-café glasses. Also known as petites flutes. Each holds about 45 ml (3 tbsp).
8 Hot drinks glasses vary in size, but have handles.

To frost a glass, moisten the edges with lemon juice, then dip in caster sugar.

Mixers and garnishes

You will need to buy mixers as you need them. Once opened they will not keep, so are not included in the overall plan for accumulating drinks.

Mixers used in this book are ginger ale, milk, soda water, beer, wine, sparkling wine, cider and champagne.

It is often the garnish that makes a cocktail look spectacular. The photographs and recipes will give you ideas for garnishing your cocktails, but look around the cocktail shops or big department stores for other ideas.

Non-alcoholic extras

Fresh ingredients should be purchased as you need them; the bitters and syrups will keep almost indefinitely, so buy and store them with your spirits.

1 Bitters: Angostura, orange, Secrestat, peach.
2 Fruit: lime, lemon, orange, pineapple, cherries (fresh and maraschino), tangerine, apple.
3 Syrups and juices: orange juice, lime cordial, grape juice, pineapple juice, lemon squash, gooseberry syrup, sirop de citron, vanilla syrup, ginger syrup, cherry syrup, orgeat syrup, fraisette (strawberry syrup), maple syrup, grenadine syrup, grapefruit juice.
4 Sugar as lump, granulated, caster, icing or syrup form.
5 Eggs.
6 Double or single cream.
7 Coconut cream.
8 Miscellaneous: blackcurrant jelly, anisette, Worcestershire sauce, tomato ketchup, lemon water, ice, sugar crystals, pickled onion, olive.

It is worth having the following most common extras to hand when mixing cocktails: Angostura and orange bitters, and grenadine.

EIGHT SIMPLE RULES OF COCKTAIL MAKING

1 Do follow the recipe, measure the ingredients and work methodically, so that you are in no doubt as to the ingredients you have or have not yet added to the shaker or mixing glass. Unless otherwise stated, each cocktail recipe provides a single drink.

2 Use bitters and syrups with care; a slight error may spoil the drink.

3 A dash is equivalent to 2 ml ($\frac{1}{3}$ tsp); there are approximately 13 dashes to the measure.

4 For shaken cocktails, place some ice in the shaker, either cracked or cubes, and add the ingredients. Replace the upper part of the shaker and holding it with both hands (one being held over the upper part to prevent accidents and spillage) shake briskly to mix and cool the ingredients. Too much shaking will melt the ice and dilute the drink. Strain into the glass. Do *not* shake sparkling drinks, such as champagne, soda water, etc.

5 For stirred or mixed cocktails, the ingredients are placed in a mixing glass with ice then stirred with a mixing spoon, briskly (unless otherwise stated), until the ingredients are mixed and cooled. Strain into the glass.

6 For blended cocktails, blend the ingredients with the specified amount of crushed ice for a few seconds (no longer or the cocktail will be too diluted). Pour into the glass.

7 Always keep a good supply of ice in the freezer or ice compartment in the refrigerator. There are ice-making appliances on the market, which are ideal for the serious cocktail maker.

8 Lemon peel is often needed to be squeezed on top of the drink. Take a thin piece of peel between the fingers and gently squeeze or twist it, so that the juice drops into the drink. The lemon peel should never be put in the glass (unless the recipe says so).

Most of the cocktail ingredients are readily available in your supermarket or off-licence, but there are a few that may be harder to trace. If you are having difficulty with any of the more unusual ingredients, we recommend:

www.thewhiskeyexchange.co.uk
www.drinks2home.co.uk
www. drinksdirect.co.uk
www.fortnumandmason.com

Occasionally, a specific brand of, for instance, rum has been recommended. If you cannot find it, you can substitute an alternative without affecting the flavour too much.

1 HOT GIN

Lemon juice	from 1 lemon
Sugar lumps	2
Dry gin	3 measures

Put the ingredients in a glass, fill up with boiling water and stir well. Serve with a slice of lemon.

2 GIMLET COCKTAIL

Dry gin	2 measures
Lime cordial	1 measure

Use the mixing glass. Serve with a slice of lime or kiwi fruit.

3 BULLDOG COOLER

Sugar syrup	1 or 2 dashes
Orange juice	from ½ orange
Dry gin	3 measures
Ginger ale	200 ml (⅓ pint)

Place a lump of ice in a tumbler, add the ingredients, stir well. Serve with a slice of orange.

4 PINK LADY COCKTAIL

Egg white	1
Grenadine	15 ml (1 tbsp)
Dry gin	3 measures

Use the shaker. Serve with a cherry.

5 ORANGE BLOSSOM COCKTAIL (1)

Orange juice	1½ measures
Dry gin	1½ measures

Use the shaker.

6 GRAPEVINE COCKTAIL

Grenadine	1 dash
Lemon juice	15 ml (1 tbsp)
Grape juice	15 ml (1 tbsp)
Dry gin	1½ measures

Use the shaker.

7 CREAM FIZZ

Sugar syrup	5 ml (1 tsp)
Lemon juice	from 1 lemon
Double cream	5 ml (1 tsp)
Dry gin	4½ measures

Use a shaker, strain into a highball glass, add ice. Top up with soda water, if desired. Stir. Serve with straws.

From left: Hot Gin, Gimlet Cocktail, Bulldog Cooler, Pink Lady Cocktail, Orange Blossom Cocktail (1), Grapevine Cocktail, Cream Fizz.

1 MARTINI COCKTAIL (SWEET)

Italian vermouth	1 measure
Dry gin	2 measures

Use the mixing glass. Serve with a little lemon peel juice squeezed on top.

2 CLOVER CLUB COCKTAIL

Lime juice	from 1 lime
or lemon juice	from ½ lemon
Egg white	1
Grenadine	1 measure
Dry gin	2 measures

Use the shaker.

3 BENNETT COCKTAIL

Angostura bitters	2 dashes
Dry gin	2 measures
Lime juice	1 measure

Use the shaker. Serve with a slice of lime.

4 VELOCITY COCKTAIL

Italian vermouth	2 measures
Dry gin	1 measure

Use the shaker. Serve with a slice of orange.

5 RAYMOND HITCH COCKTAIL

Orange juice	from ½ orange
Orange bitters	1 dash
Italian vermouth	3 measures

Use the shaker. Serve with a slice of pineapple.

6 PINK ROSE COCKTAIL

Grenadine	5 ml (1 tsp)
Egg white	1
Lemon juice	5 ml (1 tsp)
Dry gin	3 measures
Double cream, sweetened with a little sugar syrup	5 ml (1 tsp)

Use the shaker. Serve with a cherry.

7 CLUB COOLER

Lemon juice	1 dash
Grenadine	1 measure
Italian vermouth	2 measures
Soda water	300 ml (½ pint)

Place a lump of ice in a tumbler. Add the ingredients, stir well. Squeeze a little lemon juice on top and serve with straws.

From left: Martini Cocktail (sweet), Clover Club Cocktail, Bennett Cocktail, Velocity Cocktail, Raymond Hitch Cocktail, Pink Rose Cocktail, Club Cooler.

ROSSO
VERMOUTH

DUBONNET

1 CIDER COCKTAIL

Angostura bitters	1 dash
Cider	4½ measures
Sugar syrup	2.5 ml (½ tsp)

Use the mixing glass, half-filled with broken ice. Stir well. Strain into a glass. Serve with a slice of lemon on top. Non-alcoholic cider may be used.

2 ALFONSO COCKTAIL

Sugar lump	1
Secrestat bitters	2 dashes
Dubonnet	3 measures
Champagne	3 measures

Put the sugar in a wine glass and add the Secrestat bitters. Add one lump of ice and the Dubonnet and stir gently. Fill up with champagne, and top with lemon peel juice.

3 DUBONNET COCKTAIL

Dubonnet	1½ measures
Dry gin	1½ measures

Use the mixing glass. Serve with a little lemon peel squeezed on top.

4 ANGOSTURA FIZZ

Sugar syrup	15 ml (1 tbsp)
Angostura bitters	1½ measures
Lemon juice	3 measures
Egg white	1

Use a shaker, strain into a highball glass, add ice. Top up with soda water, if desired. Stir. Serve with straws.

5 GIN SLING

Dry gin	4½ measures
Sugar syrup	to taste

Put the ingredients in a tumbler containing a lump of ice. Fill up with water or soda water, as desired.

6 CAFÉ ROYAL APPETISER COCKTAIL

Orange juice	from ½ orange
Dubonnet	1½ measures
Dry gin	1½ measures

Use the shaker. Serve with a slice of orange.

7 ROYAL COCKTAIL

Angostura bitters	1 dash
Orange bitters	1 dash
Dubonnet	1 measure
Dry gin	2 measures

Use the mixing glass. Serve with a cherry and a little lemon peel juice squeezed on top.

Clockwise from left: Cider Cocktail, Alfonso Cocktail, Dubonnet Cocktail, Angostura Fizz, Gin Sling, Café Royal Appetiser Cocktail, Royal Cocktail (centre).

1 MARTINI COCKTAIL (DRY)

Orange bitters	1 dash
Dry gin	2 measures
Martini vermouth (dry)	1 measure

Use the mixing glass. Serve with a little lemon peel juice squeezed on top and a slice of lemon.

2 QUEEN'S COCKTAIL

Crushed pineapple	1 slice
French vermouth	15 ml (1 tbsp)
Italian vermouth	15 ml (1 tbsp)
Dry gin	1½ measures

Use the mixing glass. Decorate with a small piece of pineapple.

3 RAC COCKTAIL

Orange bitters	1 dash
Grenadine	1 dash
French vermouth	15 ml (1 tbsp)
Italian vermouth	15 ml (1 tbsp)
Dry gin	1½ measures

Use the mixing glass. Serve with a cherry and a little orange peel juice squeezed on top.

4 ROYAL FIZZ

Sugar syrup or grenadine	5 ml (1 tsp)
Lemon juice	from 1 lemon
Egg	1
Dry gin	4½ measures

Use a shaker. Strain into a highball glass, add ice. Top up with soda water. Serve with straws.

5 YELLOW RATTLER COCKTAIL

Orange juice	15 ml (1 tbsp)
French vermouth	15 ml (1 tbsp)
Italian vermouth	15 ml (1 tbsp)
Dry gin	15 ml (1 tbsp)

Use the shaker. Serve with a small crushed pickled onion.

6 POLO COCKTAIL

Lime juice	from ½ lime
or lemon juice	from ¼ lemon
French vermouth	2 measures
Italian vermouth	1 measure
Dry gin	2 measures

Use the shaker. Serve with a slice of lemon.

7 ORANGE BLOSSOM COCKTAIL (2)

Orange bitters	1 dash
Grenadine	1 dash
Orange juice	1½ measures
Dry gin	1½ measures

Use the shaker. Serve with a small slice of orange.

From left: Martini Cocktail (dry), Queen's Cocktail, RAC Cocktail, Royal Fizz, Yellow Rattler Cocktail, Polo Cocktail, Orange Blossom Cocktail (2).

1 AFFINITY COCKTAIL

Angostura bitters	2 dashes
French vermouth	1 measure
Italian vermouth	1 measure
Scotch whisky	1 measure

Use the mixing glass. Serve with a cherry and a little lemon peel juice squeezed on top.

2 THISTLE COCKTAIL

Angostura bitters	2 dashes
Italian vermouth	1½ measures
Scotch whisky	1½ measures

Use the mixing glass.

3 SCOTCH MIST COCKTAIL

Scotch whisky	2 measures

Use old-fashioned glasses. Shake the Scotch whisky with cracked ice and pour unstrained. Add a twist of lemon peel. Serve with straws.

4 WEMBLEY COCKTAIL

Pineapple juice	1 measure
French vermouth	1 measure
Scotch whisky	1 measure

Use the shaker.

5 WHISKY COOLER

Orange bitters	2 dashes
Scotch whisky	3 measures
Soda water	300 ml (½ pint)

Place a lump of ice in a tumbler, add the ingredients and stir well. Serve with a slice of orange. If you want to make it sweeter, include one or two dashes of sugar syrup.

6 GAELIC COFFEE

Hot coffee	1 serving
Sugar	10 ml (2 tsp)
Scotch whisky	2 measures
Double cream	to taste

Pour the coffee into a glass, then stir in the sugar and whisky. Pour the cream very gently over the back of a warmed spoon. Do not stir.

7 WHISKY TODDY

Sugar	5 ml (1 tsp)
Scotch whisky	4½ measures

Dissolve the sugar in hot water, and add the whisky. Fill up with boiling water. Serve with a slice of lemon on top.

THE FAMOUS GROUSE

Clockwise from left: Affinity Cocktail, Thistle Cocktail, Scotch Mist Cocktail, Wembley Cocktail, Whisky Cooler, Gaelic Coffee, Whisky Toddy.

PERNOD

1 NICK'S OWN COCKTAIL

Angostura bitters	1 dash
Pernod	1 dash
Italian vermouth	1½ measures

Use the mixing glass. Serve with a cherry and a little lemon peel juice squeezed on top.

2 WHITE-HORSE DAISY

Grenadine	2 dashes
Lemon juice	3 measures
Pernod	5 ml (1 tsp)
Egg white	1
White Horse whisky	3 measures

Shake well and strain. Serve in an ice-filled tumbler. Top up with soda water. Stir and decorate with fruit.

3 DUCHESS COCKTAIL

Italian vermouth	1 measure
Pernod	1 measure
French vermouth (or dry Martini)	1 measure

Use the mixing glass.

4 WHIZ-BANG COCKTAIL

Pernod	2 dashes
Grenadine	2 dashes
Orange bitters	2 dashes
French vermouth	1 measure
Scotch whisky	2 measures

Use the mixing glass. Serve with a slice of orange.

5 BELMONT COCKTAIL

Sweetened single cream	5 ml (1 tsp)
Grenadine	1 measure
Dry gin	2 measures

Use the shaker.

6 APPETISER COCKTAIL

Pernod	1 dash
Dubonnet	1½ measures
Dry gin	1½ measures

Use the shaker. Serve with a little lemon peel juice squeezed on top.

7 TIGER'S TAIL COCKTAIL

Pernod	2 measures
Orange juice	4 measures
Orange	1 slice

Serve over ice. Use an old-fashioned glass (a small tumbler).

From left: Nick's Own Cocktail, White Horse Daisy, Duchess Cocktail, Whiz-bang Cocktail, Belmont Cocktail, Appetiser Cocktail, Tiger's Tail Cocktail.

< This Week's Buy   **WEEK 7**

1 PLAIN EGGNOG

Egg	1
Sugar syrup	5 ml (1 tsp)
Brandy or rum	4½ measures
Milk	4½ measures

Prepare in a shaker, half-filled with broken ice. Strain into a glass. Sprinkle with grated nutmeg. Stir in more milk, if desired.

2 CIDER CUP (1)

Cider, preferably chilled	1.12 litres (2 pints)
Soda water, preferably chilled	100 ml (4 fl oz)
Brandy	6 measures
Lemon juice	from 1 lemon

Pour ingredients over ice in a jug and stir. Decorate with orange. Serve immediately. Serves 4

3 VALENTINE'S CHAMPAGNE COCKTAIL

Sugar lump	1
Angostura bitters	2 dashes
Lemon peel	2 pieces
Champagne	to taste

Put the lump sugar in a glass, add the Angostura bitters. Squeeze the juice of one piece of lemon peel into the glass. Add an ice cube, fill with champagne. Stir gently, squeeze the juice of the other piece of lemon peel on top.

4 LINSTEAD COCKTAIL

Pernod	1 dash
Scotch whisky	1½ measures
Sweetened pineapple juice	1½ measures

Use the shaker. Serve with a little lemon peel juice squeezed on top.

5 WASHINGTON COCKTAIL

Angostura bitters	2 dashes
Sugar syrup	2 dashes
Brandy	1 measure
French vermouth	2 measures

Use the mixing glass.

6 PRESTO COCKTAIL

Pernod	4 dashes
Orange juice	2 measures
Italian vermouth	2 measures
Brandy	8 measures

Use the mixing glass. Serve with a slice of orange each. Serves 4.

7 CHARLES COCKTAIL

Angostura bitters	1 dash
Italian vermouth	1½ measures
Brandy	1½ measures

Use the mixing glass.

Clockwise from left: Plain Eggnog, Cider Cup (1), Valentine's Champagne Cocktail, Linstead Cocktail, Washington Cocktail, Presto Cocktail, Charles Cocktail.

COINTREAU

1 MONKEY GLAND COCKTAIL

Pernod	2 dashes
Grenadine	2 dashes
Orange juice	1 measure
Dry gin	2 measures

Use the shaker. Serve with a kumquat or a cocktail cherry.

2 EGG SOUR

Egg	1
Cointreau	1 measure
Brandy	1½ measures
Lemon juice	3 dashes
Sugar or sugar syrup	to taste

Prepare the shaker, half-filled with broken ice. Shake well and strain into a glass.

3 HULA-HULA COCKTAIL

Cointreau	1 or 2 dashes
Orange juice	1 measure
Dry gin	1 measure

Use the shaker.

4 LUIGI COCKTAIL

Grenadine	5 ml (1 tsp)
Cointreau	1 dash
Tangerine juice	from ½ tangerine
French vermouth	1½ measures
Dry gin	1½ measures

Use the shaker. Serve with a little lemon peel juice squeezed and served on top.

5 CLARET CUP

Claret, preferably chilled	1 bottle
Soda water, preferably chilled	100 ml (4 fl oz)
Cointreau	1½ measures
Brandy	3 measures
Lemon juice	5 ml (1 tsp)

Place a large piece of ice in a glass jug or bowl, add the ingredients and stir well. Decorate with fruit. Serve immediately. Serves 4.

6 WYOMING SWING COCKTAIL

Orange juice	from ¼ orange
Caster sugar	2.5 ml (½ tsp)
French vermouth	1½ measures
Italian vermouth	1½ measures

Use the mixing glass. Serve in a wine glass and top with soda water.

7 ROLLS-ROYCE COCKTAIL

Brandy	1 measure
Cointreau	1 measure
Orange juice	1 measure
Egg white	1

Use the shaker.

From left: Monkey Gland Cocktail, Egg Sour, Hula-hula Cocktail, Luigi Cocktail, Claret Cup, Wyoming Swing Cocktail, Rolls-Royce Cocktail.

CRÈME CRÈME
DE MENTHE

1 MORNING GLORY FIZZ

Sugar syrup	2.5 ml (½ tsp)
Lemon juice	from ½ lemon
Egg white	1
Pernod	2 dashes
Scotch whisky	4½ measures

Use a shaker, strain into a highball glass, add ice. Top up with soda water, if desired. Sir. Serve with straws.

2 GLAD EYE COCKTAIL

Crème de menthe	1 measure
Pernod	2 measures

Use the shaker.

3 BRANDY SOUR

Sugar syrup	5 ml (1 tsp)
Brandy	3 measures
Lemon juice	from ½ lemon
or lemon and lime juice	in equal parts

Mix in a shaker, half-filled with broken ice. Strain into a small wine glass or a brandy glass. If desired, add a little soda water and decorate with fruit, e.g. lemon or lime slices.

4 ORANGES AND LEMONS COCKTAIL

Orange	1
Lemon	1
Cherries	2 or 3
Crème de menthe	1 dash
Icing sugar	10 ml (2 tsp)

Peel the orange and lemon, separate into sections and place in a sundae glass. Put the cherries in the middle, add the crème de menthe. Serve with icing sugar on top. To frost the glass, moisten the edges of glass with crème de menthe, then dip in caster sugar.

5 THIRD DEGREE COCKTAIL

Pernod	4 dashes
French vermouth	1 measure
Dry gin	2 measures

Use the mixing glass. Serve with an olive.

6 JOURNALIST COCKTAIL

Lemon juice	2 dashes
Cointreau	2 dashes
Angostura bitters	1 dash
French vermouth	½ measures
Italian vermouth	½ measure
Dry gin	2 measures

Use the shaker. Serve with a slice of orange and lemon.

7 ALEXANDER'S SISTER COCKTAIL

Crème de menthe	15 ml (1 tbsp)
Sweetened single cream	15 ml (1 tbsp)
Dry gin	1 measure

Use the shaker.

From left: Morning Glory Fizz, Glad Eye Cocktail, Brandy Sour, Oranges and Lemons Cocktail, Third Degree Cocktail, Journalist Cocktail, Alexander's Sister Cocktail.

DRY SHERRY

1 ALE POSSET

Milk	600 ml (1 pint)
Sherry	240 ml (8 fl oz)
Bitter beer	240 ml (8 fl oz)
Sugar lumps	4

Heat the milk until it almost boils. Meanwhile mix the sherry, beer and sugar in a jug, and to this add the hot milk. Serve with grated nutmeg. Serves 3.

2 ROC-A-COE COCKTAIL

Sherry	1½ measures
Dry gin	1½ measures

Use the mixing glass. Serve with a cherry.

3 ADDINGTON COCKTAIL

French vermouth	1½ measures
Italian vermouth	1½ measures

Use the mixing glass. Serve in a wine glass, top with soda, squeeze a little orange peel juice and serve on top.

4 BRAZIL COCKTAIL

Angostura bitters	1 dash
Pernod	1 dash
French vermouth	1½ measures
Dry sherry	1½ measures

Use the mixing glass. Serve with a little lemon peel juice squeezed on top.

5 GRAPEFRUIT AND ORANGEADE

Grapefruit juice	from 2 grapefruits
Orange juice	6 measures
Cider (or apple juice)	6 measures
Granulated sugar	100 g (4 oz)
Soda water	to taste

Rub the sugar on the rind of the grapefruits and oranges and put into a jug. Strain over the grapefruit and orange juice. Stir to dissolve the sugar. Just prior to serving, add the cider or apple juice, soda water and ice. Decorate with slices of fruit.

6 WHIZ-BANG COOLER

Dry gin	3 measures
Ginger ale	300 ml (½ pint)
Créme de menthe	1 dash

Place a lump of ice in a tumbler, add the ingredients and stir well. Serve with a sprig of mint of top.

7 ROB ROY COCKTAIL

Scotch whisky	1 measure
Sweet vermouth	1 measure
Angostura bitters	1 dash

Use the mixing glass. Add a cherry.

Clockwise from left: Ale Posset, Roc-a-coe Cocktail, Addington Cocktail, Brazil Cocktail, Grapefruit and Orangeade, Whiz-bang Cooler, Rob Roy Cocktail.

GREEN CHARTREUSE

1 CHAMPS ELYSÉES COCKTAIL

Angostura bitters	1 dash
Green Chartreuse	15 ml (1 tbsp)
Sweetened lemon juice	15 ml (1 tbsp)
Brandy	1½ measures

Use the shaker.

2 ORANGE FIZZ

Sugar syrup	5 ml (1 tsp)
Orange juice	from 1 orange
Dry gin	4½ measures

Use a shaker, strain into a highball glass, add ice. Top up with soda water, stir. Serve with straws and a slice of orange.

3 BRANDY DAISY

Grenadine	1½ measures
Lemon juice	3 measures
Lime juice	3 measures
Brandy	3 measures

Shake well, and strain into an ice-filled tumbler. Top up with soda water. Stir and decorate with fruit. Alternative, use half quantities of the ingredients and serve strained into an ice-filled wine glass, omitting the soda water. Decorate with fruit.

4 MOSELLE COBBLER

Sugar syrup	3 or 4 dashes
Lemon juice	1 or 2 dashes
Brandy	4 dashes
Moselle	6 measures

Make in a shaker, half-filled with broken ice. Strain into a tumbler half-full of broken ice. Serve with a straw.

5 ST GERMAIN COCKTAIL

Lemon juice	from ½ lemon
Grapefruit juice	from ¼ grapefruit
Egg white	1
Green Chartreuse	3 measures

Use the shaker.

6 PUSSY FOOT COCKTAIL

Orange juice	2 measures
Lemon juice	2 measures
Lime juice	2 measures
Grenadine	1 dash
Egg yolk	1

Use the shaker.

7 EMERALD COOLER

Lemon juice	from ½ lemon
Brandy	3 measures
Crème de menthe	1½ measures
Pineapple juice	6 measures

Stir the ingredients in a tumbler and add ice. Serve with straws.

Clockwise from top left: Champs Elysées Cocktail, Orange Fizz, Brandy Daisy, Moselle Cobbler, St Germain Cocktail, Pussy Foot Cocktail, Emerald Cooler.

CANADIAN CLUB WHISKY

1 SOUL'S KISS COCKTAIL

Orange juice	2 measures
Dubonnet	2 measures
French vermouth	4 measures
Canadian club whisky	4 measures

Use the shaker. Serve with slices of orange. Serves 4.

2 ROCK AND RYE COCKTAIL

Sugar crystals	5 ml (1 tsp)
Canadian club whisky	3 measures
Lemon juice	from 1 lemon

Dissolve the sugar crystals in the whisky and add the lemon juice.

3 CAFÉ DE PARIS COCKTAIL

Anisette or Pernod	3 dashes
Egg white	1
Sugar syrup	1 dash
Single cream	5 ml (1 tsp)
Dry gin	3 measures

Use the shaker.

4 BLACK VELVET COCKTAIL

Half-chilled Guinness	300 ml (½ pint)
Half-chilled dry champagne	300 ml (½ pint)

Add the Guinness to the champagne. Serve in 300 ml (½ pint) measures. Serves 2.

5 NEW YORK COOLER

Lemon squash	1½ measures
Grenadine	3 dashes
Canadian club whisky	3 measures
Soda water	200 ml (⅓ pint)

Place a lump of ice in a tumbler and add the ingredients. Stir well. Squeeze a little lemon peel on top and serve with a slice of lemon.

6 LOS ANGELES COCKTAIL

Italian vermouth	1 dash
Lemon juice	from 1 lemon
Egg	1
Sugar	20 ml (4 tsp)
Canadian club whisky	12 measures

Use the shaker. Serves 4.

7 MOUNTAIN COCKTAIL

Egg white	1
Lemon juice	½ measure
French vermouth	½ measure
Italian vermouth	½ measure
Canadian club whisky	1½ measures

Use the shaker.

Clockwise from left: Soul's Kiss Cocktail, Rock and Rye Cocktail, Café de Paris Cocktail, Black Velvet Cocktail, New York Cooler, Los Angeles Cocktail, Mountain Cocktail.

WHITE RUM

1 SPRING SHAKE-UP

Grenadine	3 dashes
Angostura bitters	1 dash
Cointreau	15 ml (1 tbsp)
White rum	1½ measures
Pineapple juice	4½ measures

Shake all the ingredients together, strain into a tumbler and add ice. Serve with straws. Decorate with a strawberry and a cherry.

2 CUBA LIBRE

Lime juice	from ½ lime
White rum	2 measures
Lime peel	from ½ lime, in one piece
Cola	to taste

Place the lime juice and peel in a tumbler, add ice and the white rum and fill up with cola. Stir before serving.

3 PIÑA COLADA

White rum	4½ measures
Pineapple juice	6 measures
Coconut cream	3 measures

Blend the ingredients with two scoops of crushed ice. Serve in an ice-filled pineapple shell or large glass. Garnish with fruit and parasols.

4 SCORPION

Brandy	15 ml (1 tbsp)
White rum	3 measures
Orange juice	15 ml (1 tbsp)
Orgeat syrup	5 ml (1 tsp)

Use the shaker. Strain into a bowl-shaped glass, half-filled with crushed ice. Garnish with a fresh flower.

5 CASABLANCA

White rum	45 ml (3 tbsp)
Pineapple juice	3 measures
Coconut cream	1½ measures
Grenadine	2 dashes

Use the shaker. Serve in a large wine glass and garnish with a cherry, a slice of orange and a slice of pineapple.

6 BACARDI CRUSTA

Sugar syrup	5 ml (1 tsp)
Lemon juice	1 measure
Angostura bitters	2 dashes
Pernod	5 ml (1 tsp)
Bacardi rum	2 measures

Make in a shaker half-filled with broken ice. Place a spiral of lemon rind in a frosted (crusta) glass, add ice and strained cocktail. To frost the glass, moisten the edges with lemon juice, then dip the rim in caster sugar.

7 RUM COOLER

Sugar syrup	5 ml (1 tsp)
Lime juice	1½ measures
White rum	3 measures
Soda water	200 ml (⅓ pint)

Place a lump of ice in a tumbler, add the ingredients, stir well. Serve with a slice of lime.

From left: Spring Shake-Up, Cuba Libre, Piña Colada, Scorpion, Casablanca, Bacardi Crusta, Rum Cooler.

VODKA

1 DANDY COCKTAIL

Angostura bitters	1 dash
Orange peel	1 piece
Cointreau	3 dashes
Dubonnet	1½ measures
Lemon peel	1 piece
Canadian club whisky	1½ measures

Use the shaker.

2 VODKATINI COCKTAIL

Vodka	2 measures
French vermouth	1 measure
Lemon peel	1 twist

Use the mixing glass.

3 BALALAIKA COCKTAIL

Vodka	1 measure
Cointreau	1 measure
Lemon juice	1 measure

Use the shaker.

4 SAND MARTIN COCKTAIL

Green Chartreuse	5 ml (1 tsp)
Italian vermouth	1½ measures
Dry gin	1½ measures

Use the mixing glass. Serve with a lemon peel juice squeezed on top.

5 BOO BOO'S SPECIAL

Orange juice	2 measures
Pineapple juice	2 measures
Lemon juice	1 dash
Angostura bitters	1 dash
Grenadine	1 dash

Use the shaker. Serve in a tumbler garnished with slices of pineapple and orange.

6 SCREWDRIVER

Vodka	2 measures
Orange juice	2 measures

Serve with ice in a frosted glass. Decorate with a slice of orange. To frost the glass, moisten the rim with orange juice, then dip in caster sugar.

7 BLOODY MARY

Vodka	2 measures
Worcestershire sauce	2 dashes
Lemon juice	1 dash
Tomato juice	to taste

Use a 6 oz (175 ml) goblet. Add ice, vodka, Worcestershire sauce, a little lemon juice. Top with tomato juice and stir with a stick of celery.

Clockwise from left: Dandy Cocktail, Vodkatini Cocktail, Balalaika Cocktail, Sand Martin Cocktail, Boo Boo's Special, Screwdriver, Bloody Mary.

CAMPARI

1 AMERICANO COCKTAIL
Campari	1 measure
Sweet vermouth	1 measure

Stir and fill with soda. Serve with ice.

2 FALLEN ANGEL COCKTAIL
Angostura bitters	1 dash
Crème de menthe	2 dashes
Lemon juice	from ½ lemon
Dry gin	3 measures

Use the shaker.

3 BACARDI COCKTAIL
Lime juice	1 measure
Bacardi rum	1 measure
Sugar syrup	to taste

Use the shaker. Serve with a slice of lime.

4 NEGRONI COCKTAIL
Dry gin	1 measure
Sweet vermouth	1 measure
Campari	1 measure

Stir. Serve with ice and half a slice of orange.

5 LADIES' COCKTAIL
Angostura bitters	2 dashes
Pernod	1 dash
Anisette	2 dashes
Canadian club whisky	3 measures

Use the mixing glass. Serve with a slice of pineapple on top.

6 TROPICAL DAWN
Dry gin	1½ measures
Orange juice	1½ measures
Campari	15 ml (1 tbsp)

Half-fill the shaker with crushed ice. Add the gin and orange juice. Shake. Pour into a glass. Pour the Campari over the top. Decorate with a slice of orange and cherries.

7 SW1 COCKTAIL
Vodka	1 measure
Campari	1 measure
Orange juice	1 measure
Egg white	1

Use the shaker. Serve with cocktail cherries.

From left: Americano Cocktail, Fallen Angel Cocktail, Bacardi Cocktail, Negroni Cocktail, Ladies' Cocktail, Tropical Dawn, SW1 Cocktail.

BLUE CURAÇAO

1 BLUE BIRD COCKTAIL

Angostura bitters	4 dashes
Blue curaçao	5 dashes
Dry gin	3 measures

Use the shaker. Serve with a cherry and a little lemon peel juice squeezed on top.

2 BLUE SOUR

Blue curaçao	3 measures
Lemon juice	from ½ lemon
Sugar syrup	5 ml (1 tsp)

Put the ingredients into a shaker, half-filled with broken ice. Shake. Strain into a frosted glass. To frost the glass, moisten rim with the curaçao, then dip in caster sugar.

3 EAST INDIA COCKTAIL

Angostura bitters	2 dashes
Pineapple juice	2 dashes
Blue curaçao	2 dashes
Brandy	3 measures

Use the shaker. Serve with a cherry and a little lemon peel juice squeezed on top.

4 TRUE BLUE

Blue curaçao	3 measures
Lime juice	1½ measures
Soda water	to taste

Serve in a tumbler with a few lumps of ice. Serve with a spiral of lime.

5 MILLIONAIRE COCKTAIL (1)

Egg white	1
Blue curaçao	2 dashes
Grenadine	1 measure
Canadian club whisky	2 measures

Use the shaker.

6 BREAKFAST EGGNOG

Egg	1
Blue curaçao	1½ measures
Brandy	4½ measures
Milk	6 measures

Prepare in a shaker, half-filled with broken ice. Strain into a glass, sprinkle with grated nutmeg. Stir in more milk if desired. If preferred, use single cream instead of milk, or mix milk and cream.

7 BOSOM CARESSER COCKTAIL

Grenadine	3 dashes
Egg yolk	1
Blue curaçao	1 measure
Brandy	2 measures

Use the shaker.

Clockwise from left: Blue Bird Cocktail, Blue Sour, East India Cocktail, True Blue, Millionaire Cocktail (1), Breakfast Eggnog, Bosom Caresser Cocktail (centre).

GALLIANO

1 OLD PAL COCKTAIL

French vermouth	1 measure
Campari	1 measure
Canadian club whisky	1 measure

Use the mixing glass.

2 MANHATTAN COCKTAIL (DRY)

Angostura bitters	2 dashes
French vermouth	1½ measures
Canadian club whisky	1½ measures

Use the mixing glass. Serve with an olive or cherry and a little lemon peel juice squeezed on top.

3 GOLDEN DREAM COCKTAIL

Galliano	2 measures
Cointreau	15 ml (1 tbsp)
Orange juice	15 ml (1 tbsp)
Double cream	15 ml (1 tbsp)

Shake and serve in a champagne glass.

4 HARVEY WALLBANGER

Vodka	2 measures
Orange juice	4 measures
Galliano	10 ml (2 tsp)

Shake and strain on to ice. Float the Galliano on top. Serve with straws.

5 SIDECAR COCKTAIL

Lemon juice	1 measure
Cointreau	1 measure
Brandy	1 measure

Use the shaker.

6 INK STREET COCKTAIL

Lemon juice	1 measure
Orange juice	1 measure
Canadian club whisky	1 measure

Use the shaker. Serve with a slice of orange and lemon.

7 BACARDI SPECIAL COCKTAIL

Grenadine	5 ml (1 tsp)
Lime juice	from ½ lime
Dry gin	1 measure
Bacardi rum	2 measures

Use the shaker. Serve with a slice of lime.

Clockwise from top left: Old Pal Cocktail, Manhattan Cocktail (Dry), Golden Dream Cocktail, Harvey Wallbanger, Sidecar Cocktail, Ink Street Cocktail, Bacardi Special Cocktail.

APRICOT BRANDY

1 CUBAN COCKTAIL

Lime juice	15 ml (1 tbsp)
Apricot brandy	15 ml (1 tbsp)
Brandy	1½ measures

Use the mixing glass. Serve with a slice of lime.

2 FAIRY BELLE COCKTAIL

Grenadine	5 ml (1 tsp)
Egg white	1
Apricot brandy	15 ml (1 tbsp)
Dry gin	45 ml (3 tbsp)

Use the shaker.

3 CHAMPAGNE COBBLER

Sugar syrup	3 or 4 dashes
Lemon juice	1 or 2 dashes
Brandy	2 dashes
Champagne	6 measures

Prepare in the mixing glass (not the shaker), half-filled with broken ice. Stir gently, and strain into a tumbler half-full of broken ice. Decorate with fruit and serve with a straw.

4 PARADISE COCKTAIL

Orange juice	1 measure
Apricot brandy	1 measure
Dry gin	1 measure

Use the shaker. Serve with a slice of orange.

5 PICCADILLY COCKTAIL

Pernod	1 dash
Grenadine	1 dash
French vermouth	1 measure
Dry gin	2 measures

Use the shaker.

6 FOURTH DEGREE COCKTAIL

Pernod	4 dashes
French vermouth	15 ml (1 tbsp)
Italian vermouth	15 ml (1 tbsp)
Dry gin	1½ measures

Use the mixing glass. Serve with a cherry.

7 GIN DAISY

Grenadine	15 ml (1 tbsp)
Lemon juice	3 measures
Dry gin	3 measures

Shake well, and strain into an ice-filled tumbler. Top up with soda water. Stir and decorate with fruit. Alternative serving: strain into an ice-filled wine glass, omit soda water. Decorate with fruit. Use half quantities for this method.

From left: Cuban Cocktail, Fairy Belle Cocktail, Champagne Cobbler, Paradise Cocktail, Piccadilly Cocktail, Fourth Degree Cocktail, Gin Daisy.

CHERRY BRANDY

1 BLOOD AND SAND COCKTAIL

Orange juice	15 ml (1 tbsp)
Italian vermouth	15 ml (1 tbsp)
Cherry brandy	15 ml (1 tbsp)
Scotch whisky	15 ml (1 tbsp)

Use the mixing glass. Serve with a slice of orange and a cherry.

2 BRANDY FIX

Sugar syrup	5 ml (1 tsp)
Lemon juice	from ½ lemon
Brandy	1½ measures
Cherry brandy	1½ measures
Water	to taste

Place ingredients in a tumbler, stir. Fill up glass with crushed ice. Decorate with fruit and serve with straws.

3 SINGAPORE SLING

Lemon juice	1 measure
Dry gin	2 measures
Cherry brandy	1 measure

Put the ingredients in a shaker, half-filled with broken ice. Shake well, and strain into an ice-filled tumbler. Fill up with soda water and stir. Serve with fruit and a parasol.

4 BRANDY SMASH

Sugar lump	½
Mint	4 sprigs
Brandy	3 measures

In the shaker dissolve the sugar in a little water. Quickly stir in the mint and remove. Half-fill the shaker with ice, add brandy, shake well, then strain. Serve in a wine glass decorated with fruit.

5 COOPERSTOWN COCKTAIL

French vermouth	1 measure
Italian vermouth	1 measure
Dry gin	1 measure
Mint	2 sprigs

Use the mixing glass. Serve with a cherry on top.

6 LONDON COCKTAIL

Orange bitters	2 dashes
Sugar syrup	2 dashes
Pernod	2 dashes
Dry gin	3 measures

Use the mixing glass. Serve with olives and a little lemon peel juice squeezed on top.

7 VANDERBILT COCKTAIL

Angostura bitters	2 dashes
Sugar syrup	3 dashes
Cherry brandy	15 ml (1 tbsp)
Brandy	15 ml (1 tbsp)

Use the mixing glass.

Top from left: Blood and Sand Cocktail, Brandy Fix, Singapore Sling, Brandy Smash.
Bottom from left: Cooperstown Cocktail, London Cocktail, Vanderbilt Cocktail.

SWEDISH PUNSCH

1 WALDORF COCKTAIL

Dry gin	1 measure
Swedish punsch	2 measures
Lime juice	from ½ lime
or lemon juice	from ¼ lemon

Use the mixing glass.

2 GREENBRIAR COCKTAIL

Peach bitters	1 dash
Dry sherry	2 measures
French vermouth	1 measure
Mint	1 sprig

Use the mixing glass.

3 FAIR AND WARMER COCKTAIL

Blue curaçao	2 dashes
Italian vermouth	1 measure
Bacardi rum	2 measures

Use the mixing glass. Serve with a cherry.

4 TANGLEFOOT COCKTAIL

Lemon juice	2 measures
Swedish punsch	4 measures
Orange juice	2 measures
Bacardi rum	4 measures

Use the shaker. Serve with a slice of orange. Serves 4.

5 MELBA COCKTAIL

Pernod	2 dashes
Grenadine	2 dashes
Swedish punsch	1½ measures
Bacardi rum	1½ measures
Lime juice	from ½ lime
or lemon juice	from ¼ lemon

Use the shaker. Serve with a slice of lime and lemon and a cherry.

6 DOCTOR COCKTAIL

Swedish punsch	2 measures
Lime or lemon juice	1 measure

Use the shaker.

7 BOOMERANG COCKTAIL

Angostura bitters	1 dash
Swedish punsch	1 measure
Lemon juice	1 dash
Canadian club whisky	1 measure
French vermouth	1 measure

Use the shaker.

From left: Waldorf Cocktail, Greenbriar Cocktail, Fair and Warmer Cocktail, Tanglefoot Cocktail, Melba Cocktail, Doctor Cocktail, Boomerang Cocktail.

CALVADOS

1	**TIPPERARY COCKTAIL**		Use the shaker. Serve with a sprig of mint.
	Grenadine	3 dashes	
	Orange juice	5 ml (1 tsp)	
	Italian vermouth	1 measure	
	Dry gin	2 measures	

2	**BENTLEY COCKTAIL**		Use the shaker. Serve with a cherry.
	Dubonnet	1½ measures	
	Calvados	1½ measures	

3	**STAR COCKTAIL**		Use the shaker. Serve with slices of apple.
	French vermouth	1 dash	
	Calvados	1½ measures	
	Italian vermouth	1 dash	
	Dry gin	1½ measures	
	Grapefruit juice	5 ml (1 tsp)	

4	**PRINCE'S SMILE COCKTAIL**		Use the shaker. Serve with a slice of lemon.
	Lemon juice	1 dash	
	Apricot brandy	15 ml (1 tbsp)	
	Calvados	15 ml (1 tbsp)	
	Dry gin	1½ measures	

5	**ANGEL FACE COCKTAIL**		Use the shaker.
	Apricot brandy	1 measure	
	Calvados	1 measure	
	Dry gin	1 measure	

6	**GINGER ALE CUP**		Non-alcoholic. Dissolve sugar in the boiling water, chill. Place a large piece of ice in a jug or bowl, add the ingredients, and stir well. Decorate with sprigs mint and fruit. Serve immediately. Serves 4.
	Granulated sugar	225 g (8 oz)	
	Boiling water	1.2 litres (2 pints)	
	Lime juice	100 ml (4 fl oz)	
	Ginger ale, chilled	100 ml (4 fl oz)	

7	**TWELVE MILES OUT COCKTAIL**		Use the mixing glass. Serve with a little lemon peel juice squeezed on top and a slice of lemon.
	Bacardi rum	1 measure	
	Swedish punsch	1 measure	
	Calvados	1 measure	

Clockwise from top left: Tipperary Cocktail, Bentley Cocktail, Star Cocktail, Prince's Smile Cocktail, Angel Face Cocktail, Ginger Ale Cup, Twelve Miles Out Cocktail.

ORANGE OR BROWN CURAÇAO

1 ROULETTE COCKTAIL

Bacardi rum	15 ml (1 tbsp)
Swedish punsch	15 ml (1 tbsp)
Calvados	1½ measures

Use the mixing glass.

2 RYE FIZZ

Grenadine	5 or 6 dashes
Lemon juice	4½ measures
Egg white	1
Canadian club whisky	3 measures
Brown or orange curaçao	5 ml (1 tsp)

Use the shaker, strain into a highball glass, add ice. Top up with soda water if desired. Serve with straws.

3 NEW YORK COCKTAIL

Sugar lump	1
Grenadine	2 dashes
Orange peel	1 piece
Canadian club whisky	3 measures
Lime juice	from 1 lime

Use the shaker. Serve with a little lemon peel juice squeezed on top.

4 WHISKY DAISY

Grenadine	1 measure
Lemon juice	3 measures
Lime juice	3 measures
Orange juice	1½ measures
Scotch whisky	3 measures

Shake and strain. Serve in an ice filled tumbler. Top up with soda water, stir and decorate. Alternative serving: strain half quantities into an ice-filled wine glass. Omit soda. Decorate with fruit.

5 CLARIDGE COCKTAIL

Apricot brandy	3 measures
Cointreau	3 measures
French vermouth	1 measure
Dry gin	1 measure

Use the shaker. Serve with a cherry.

6 RUM DAISY

Grenadine	15 ml (1 tbsp)
Lemon juice	3 measures
Brown or orange curaçao	2 or 3 dashes
White rum	3 measures

Shake well, and strain into an ice-filled tumbler. Top up with soda water. Stir and decorate with fruit. Alternatively, use half quantities, omitting the soda water, strain into an ice-filled wine glass and decorate with fruit.

7 WHITE COCKTAIL

Orange bitters	2 dashes
Dry gin	3 measures
Anisette	6 dashes
or Pernod and sugar syrup	1 dash

Use the mixing glass. Serve with lemon peel juice squeezed on top.

From left: Roulette Cocktail, Rye Fizz, New York Cocktail, Whisky Daisy, Claridge Cocktail, Rum Daisy, White Cocktail.

CRÈME DE CASSIS/PORT

1 ROOSEVELT COCKTAIL

Dry gin	1 measure
White rum	1 measure
Lemon juice	1 measure
Grenadine	1 measure

Use the shaker.

2 PARISIAN COCKTAIL

French vermouth	1 measure
Crème de cassis	1 measure
Dry gin	1 measure

Use the mixing glass. Serve in a frosted glass if desired. To frost the glass, moisten the rim with crème de cassis, then dip in caster sugar.

3 PORT WINE COCKTAIL

Brandy	1 dash
Port	3 measures

Use the mixing glass. Serve with a little orange peel juice squeezed on top and a slice of orange.

4 KIR COCKTAIL

Dry white wine, chilled	1 glass
Crème de cassis	5 ml (1 tsp)

With a teaspoon, float crème de cassis on the wine.

5 DEMPSEY COCKTAIL

Pernod	2 dashes
Grenadine	3 dashes
Calvados	2 measures
Dry gin	1 measure

Use the shaker. Serve with cherries.

6 CALVADOS COCKTAIL

Orange juice	4 measures
Cointreau	2 measures
Orange bitters	2 measures
Calvados	4 measures

Use the shaker. Serve with a slice of orange and apple. Serves 4.

7 PORT WINE SANGAREE

Sugar	5 ml (1 tsp)
Water	3 measures
Port	6 measures

Dissolve the sugar in water in a tumbler, add the port and fill with crushed ice. Stir well, decorate with grated nutmeg and fruit if desired.

From left: Roosevelt Cocktail, Parisian Cocktail, Port Wine Cocktail, Kir Cocktail, Dempsey Cocktail, Calvados Cocktail, Port Wine Sangaree.

CRÈME DE CASSIS

1 MISSISSIPPI MULE

Lemon juice	2 measures
Crème de cassis	2 measures
Dry gin	8 measures

Use the shaker. Serves 4.

2 GRAPE COCKTAIL

Angostura bitters	1 dash
Grape juice	1½ measures
Sugar syrup	3 measures
Soda water	6 measures

Use the mixing glass, half-filled with broken ice. Add the bitters, grape juice and sugar syrup. Stir well, and strain into a tumbler. Fill with soda, and decorate with fruit.

3 PINEAPPLE LEMONADE

Pineapple chunks	1 small tin
Lemon rind and juice	from 2 lemons
Granulated sugar	100 g (4 oz)

Non-alcoholic. Place the lemon rind in a jug. Liquidise the pineapple and add with 600 ml (1 pint) of boiling water. Mix lemon juice with sugar and pour in. Strain. Add soda water and ice.

4 HAWAIIAN COCKTAIL

Dry gin	2 measures
Orange juice	2 measures
Cointreau	1 dash

Shake.

5 CASSIS HIGHBALL

Dry gin	1 measure
Crème de cassis	1 measure
Sparkling apple juice	to taste

Use the mixing glass for the gin and crème de cassis. Serve in a tumbler with a few lumps of ice and fill up with apple juice. Decorate with a slice of apple.

6 ICED TEA

Tea leaves	5 ml (1 tsp)
Water	300 ml (½ pint
Sugar	to taste
Lemon slices	to taste
Fruit juice	to taste

Non-alcoholic. Make the tea in the usual way. Allow it to draw, then strain and leave to cool. Add sugar, lemon slices and fruit juice to taste, then stand the tea on ice until required. Serve with small ice cubes.

7 GRAPEFRUIT COCKTAIL (1)

Grapefruit	1
Bananas	2
Pineapple chunks	1 small tin
Sherry	6 measures

Press the grapefruit flesh through a sieve. Slice the bananas and pineapple thinly and add to the grapefruit purée. Sprinkle caster sugar on the fruit and pour the sherry over it. Stand on ice for an hour. Serve in a sherbet glass.

Clockwise from top left: Mississippi Mule, Grape Cocktail, Pineapple Lemonade, Hawaiian Cocktail, Cassis Highball, Iced Tea, Grapefruit Cocktail (1).

PLYMOUTH GIN

1 'SG' COCKTAIL

Grenadine	3 dashes
Lemon juice	1 measure
Orange juice	1 measure
Canadian club whisky	1 measure

Use the shaker.

2 BIJOU COCKTAIL

Orange bitters	1 dash
Plymouth gin	1 measure
Green Chartreuse	1 measure
Italian vermouth	1 measure

Use the mixing glass. Serve with a cherry and a little lemon peel juice squeezed on top.

3 GIN FIX

Sugar syrup	2 tsp
Lemon juice	from ½ lemon
Dry gin	4½ measures
Water	to taste

Place ingredients in a tumbler. Fill up the glass with crushed ice. Decorate with fruit and serve with straws.

4 DEPTH CHARGE COCKTAIL

Lemon juice	4 dashes
Grenadine	2 dashes
Calvados	1½ measures
Brandy	1½ measures

Use the shaker.

5 PINK GIN COCKTAIL

Angostura bitters	1 dash
Plymouth gin	3 measures

Use the shaker.

6 CHAMPAGNE JULEP

Sugar lump	1
Mint	2 sprigs
Chilled champagne	

Put the sugar in a champagne glass, add the mint and gently crush the leaves with a spoon. Fill with champagne. Stir gently. Decorate with seasonal fruit and mint.

7 OLIVETTE COCKTAIL

Pernod	3 dashes
Orange bitters	2 dashes
Sugar syrup	2 dashes
Plymouth gin	3 measures

Use the mixing glass. Serve with an olive and a little lemon peel juice squeezed on top.

From left: 'SG' Cocktail, Bijou Cocktail, Gin Fix, Depth Charge Cocktail, Pink Gin Cocktail, Champagne Julep, Olivette Cocktail.

TEQUILA

1 STRAWBERRY DAWN

Dry gin	2 measures
Coconut cream	2 measures
Strawberries	3
Crushed ice	2 scoops

Blend for a few seconds. Serve in a large glass.

2 BLOODHOUND COCKTAIL

Crushed strawberries	3
French vermouth	15 ml (1 tbsp)
Italian vermouth	15 ml (1 tbsp)
Dry gin	1½ measures

Use the shaker. Serve with a strawberry.

3 TEQUILA SUNRISE

Tequila	2 measures
Orange juice	4 measures
Grenadine	1 dash

Shake the tequila and orange juice together well. Pour into the glass. Add a dash of grenadine. Serve with straws.

4 MARGARITA

Tequila	2 measures
Lemon juice	2 measures
Cointreau	1 measure

Shake. Frost the rim of the glass with salt.

5 STRAWBERRY CREAM COOLER

Dry gin	3 measures
Lemon juice	1½ measures
Single cream	4½ measures
Strawberry	1
Sugar	5 ml (1 tsp)

Blend for a few seconds. Pour into a tumbler and add soda water and ice cubes. Garnish with strawberries.

6 AMERICAN BEAUTY COCKTAIL

Crème de menthe	1 dash
French vermouth	15 ml (1 tbsp)
Orange juice	15 ml (1 tbsp)
Brandy	15 ml (1 tbsp)
Grenadine	15 ml (1 tbsp)
Port	1 dash

Use the shaker. Serve with a little port on top and a slice of orange.

7 BRANDY JULEP

Mint	4 sprigs
Caster sugar	5 ml (1 tsp)
Brandy	4½ measures

Cover the mint with sugar in a tumbler. Add enough water to dissolve the sugar. Crush the mint gently. Add the brandy and fill the glass with broken ice. Stir. Decorate with mint and fruit.

From left: Strawberry Dawn, Bloodhound Cocktail, Tequila Sunrise, Margarita, Strawberry Cream Cooler, American Beauty Cocktail, Brandy Julep.

CRÈME DE BANANE

1 COMMODORE COCKTAIL

Orange bitters	3 dashes
Sugar syrup	3 dashes
Lime juice	from ½ lime
Canadian club whisky	3 measures

Use the shaker. Serve with a slice of lemon and lime.

2 BANANA DAIQUIRI

White rum	3 measures
Crème de banane	1½ measures
Lime juice	from ½ lime
Banana	½

Blend for a few seconds with two scoops of crushed ice. Serve in a large wine glass.

3 CHERRY BLOSSOM COCKTAIL

Grenadine	1 dash
Cherry brandy	1½ measures
Orange curaçao	1 dash
Brandy	1½ measures
Lemon juice	1 dash

Use the shaker. Serve very cold, with a fresh cherry.

4 BARRACUDA

White rum	3 measures
Sugar syrup	2 dashes
Galliano	1½ measures
Lime juice	from ½ lime
Pineapple juice	3 measures
Champagne	to taste

Use the shaker for all the ingredients except the champagne. Serve in a pineapple shell and top with champagne.

5 QUARTER DECK COCKTAIL

Lime juice	5 ml (1 tsp)
Dry sherry	1 measure
Rum	2 measures

Use the mixing glass.

6 BANANA BLISS

Crème de banane	1½ measures
Orange juice	15 ml (1 tbsp)
White rum	1½ measures
Angostura bitters	1 dash
Single cream	1½ measures
Grenadine	1 dash

Use the shaker for all the ingredients except the grenadine. Strain into a tumbler. Add the grenadine.

7 HOT DECK COCKTAIL

Jamaica ginger	1 dash
Italian vermouth	15 ml (1 tbsp)
Canadian club whisky	3 measures

Use the mixing glass.

Clockwise from bottom left: Commodore Cocktail, Banana Daiquiri, Cherry Blossom Cocktail, Barracuda, Quarter Deck Cocktail, Banana Bliss, Hot Deck Cocktail.

CALVADOS

1 SHANDY GAFF

Bitter beer, chilled	300 ml (½ pint)
Ginger ale, chilled	300 ml (½ pint)

Mix in a tumbler and serve ice cold, decorated with fruit. Serves 3.

2 CALVADOS HIGHBALL

Calvados	4½ measures
Soda water or ginger ale	to taste

Pour into a tumbler with a few lumps of ice. Serve with a piece of lemon peel or a slice of lemon.

3 CALVADOS RABBIT COCKTAIL

Lemon juice	2 measures
Maple syrup	4 measures
Orange juice	2 measures
Calvados	4 measures

Use the shaker. Serve with slices of orange and lemon and a cherry. Serves 4.

4 SUNDEW COCKTAIL

Angostura bitters	1 dash
Sugar syrup	1½ measures
Grape juice	1½ measures
Orange juice	3 measures
Orange	2 slices
Calvados	4½ measures

Use the mixing glass. Stir well, and strain into a glass. Fill up with soda water, and decorate with fruit.

5 JACK ROSE COCKTAIL

Lime juice	from 1 lime
or lemon juice	from ½ lemon
Calvados	45 ml (3 tbsp)
Grenadine	15 ml (1 tbsp)

Use the shaker.

6 CALVADOS SOUR

Sugar syrup	2 dashes
Grenadine	1 dash
Lemon juice	from ½ lemon
or lemon and lime juice	in equal parts
Calvados	3 measures

Mix in a shaker, half-filled with broken ice. Strain into a small wine glass. Add a little soda water, and decorate with apple slices.

7 THIRD RAIL COCKTAIL

Pernod	1 dash
Calvados	1 measure
Brandy	1 measure
Bacardi rum	1 measure

Use the shaker.

Clockwise from bottom left: Shandy Gaff, Calvados Highball, Calvados Rabbit Cocktail, Sundew Cocktail, Jack Rose Cocktail, Calvados Sour, Third Rail Cocktail (centre).

GIN

1 ICED CHOCOLATE

Hot chocolate	6000 ml (1 pint)
Vanilla ice cream	to taste

Non-alcoholic. Make the hot chocolate in the normal way, and allow it to cool, then stand in a jug surrounded with ice or put in the refrigerator. When required, serve in small glasses topped with vanilla ice cream.

2 BLACKCURRANT COCKTAIL

Grapefruit	½
Blackcurrants	50 g (2 oz)
Gin	1 measure (optional)
Icing sugar	10 ml (2 tsp)

Cut round and through to separate the grapefruit segments, then cut a hole in the middle and fill with blackcurrants. Pour over the gin, if you like. Serve with icing sugar and a spoon.

3 EGG LEMONADE

Lemon juice	from 1 lemon
Caster sugar	15 ml (1 tbsp)
Egg	1

Non-alcoholic. Prepare in the mixing glass, stir well and strain into tumbler. Serve with water or soda water.

4 MIXED FRUIT COCKTAIL

Blackcurrants, raspberries and strawberries	in equal quantities
Sugar	to taste
Lemon juice	to taste

Non-alcoholic. Mash the fruits well and add the sugar. Strain into the shaker, half-filled with broken ice, and add the lemon juice and a little water. Shake, then strain into a wine glass.

5 ORANGEADE

Oranges	4
Lemons	2
Granulated sugar	1 kg (2 lb)

Non-alcoholic. Remove the zest from the oranges and lemons as thinly as possible. Put in a jug with the sugar and pour 2.25 litres (4 pints) of boiling water over it. Add the juice of the oranges and lemons, stir well, and cool. Strain and serve with fruit.

6 RASPBERRY LEMONADE

Raspberries	450 g (1 lb)
Lemons	2
Caster sugar	100 g (4 oz)

Non-alcoholic. Press the raspberries through a sieve, add the juice of the lemons and the sugar, stir well, and mix 1.2 litres (2 pints) of cold water. Serve with ice and decorate with raspberries.

7 CHERRY COCKTAIL

Angostura bitters	1 dash
Lime juice	2 dashes
Ginger syrup	1½ measures
Cherry syrup	1½ measures
Soda water	6 measures

Use the mixing glass, half-filled with broken ice. Add all except the soda water, stir and strain into a tumbler. Fill up with soda water and decorate with fruit.

Clockwise from left: Iced Chocolate, Blackcurrant Cocktail, Egg Lemonade, Mixed Fruit Cocktail, Orangeade, Raspberry Lemonade, Cherry Cocktail.

MARASCHINO/
YELLOW CHARTREUSE

1 DEPTH BOMB COCKTAIL
Lemon juice	1 dash
Grenadine	4 dashes
Calvados	1½ measures
Brandy	1½ measures

Use the shaker.

2 ALLEN (SPECIAL) COCKTAIL
Lemon juice	1 dash
Maraschino	1 measure
Plymouth gin	2 measures

Use the shaker. Serve with a cherry.

3 YELLOW PARROT COCKTAIL
Pernod	1 measure
Yellow Chartreuse	1 measure
Apricot brandy	1 measure

Use the shaker.

4 CHOCOLATE COCKTAIL (1)
Drinking chocolate powder	5 ml (1 tsp)
Egg yolk	1
Yellow Chartreuse	1½ measures
Port	1½ measures

Use the shaker. Serve with a flake chocolate bar.

5 GOLDEN SLIPPER
Egg yolk	1
Yellow Chartreuse	1 measure
Brandy	1 measure

Add the ingredients in the stated order, pouring the liquids over the back of a spoon so that they touch the sides of the glass. Serve in a pousse-café glass. Do not stir, a layered effect should be achieved.

6 RUM CRUSTA
Sugar syrup	5 ml (1 tsp)
Lemon juice	1 measure
Angostura bitters	2 dashes
Maraschino	5 ml (1 tsp)
White or dark rum	2 measures

Use the shaker. Place a spiral of lemon rind in a frosted (crusta) glass, add ice and strained cocktail. Decorate with seasonal fruit.

7 CIDER CUP (2)
Cointreau	2 measures
Maraschino	1½ measures
Brandy	3 measures
Dry sherry	4½ measures
Lemon tea	5 ml (1 tsp)
Cider, chilled	1.2 litres (2 pints)

Place a large piece of ice in a glass jug or bowl. Add the ingredients, stir well, and decorate with fruit and sprigs mint. Serves 4.

Clockwise from left: Depth Bomb Cocktail, Allen (Special) Cocktail, Yellow Parrot Cocktail, Chocolate Cocktail (1), Golden Slipper, Rum Crusta, Cider Cup (2).

YELLOW CHARTREUSE

1 GRAPEFRUIT DRINK

Oranges	3
Grapefruit	1
Granulated sugar	100 g (4 oz)
Soda water, chilled	100 ml (4 fl oz)

Non-alcoholic. Remove the orange zest and put into a jug with the sugar. Add 600 ml (1 pint) of water, the strained juice of the oranges and grapefruit. Strain, add a lump of ice and soda water.

2 WHITE ROSE COCKTAIL

Orange juice	from ¼ orange
Lime juice	from ½ lime
Egg white	1
Maraschino	15 ml (1 tbsp)
Dry gin	3 tbsp

Use the shaker. Serve with seasonal fruit.

3 CHOCOLATE COCKTAIL (2)

Hot chocolate powder	5 ml (1 tsp)
Egg	1
Yellow Chartreuse	1½ measures
Maraschino	1½ measures

Use the shaker.

4 SHERRY SANGAREE

Caster sugar	5 ml (1 tsp)
Water	3 measures
Dry sherry	4½ measures

Dissolve sugar in the water in a tumbler, add sherry and fill with crushed ice. Stir well, decorate with grated nutmeg and cherries.

5 TUXEDO COCKTAIL

Pernod	1 dash
Maraschino	1 dash
Orange bitters	2 dashes
French vermouth	1½ measures
Dry gin	1½ measures

Use the mixing glass. Serve with grapes, slices of banana and a little lemon peel juice squeezed on top.

6 ICED COFFEE

Strong fresh coffee	12 measures
Sugar	to taste
Vanilla-flavoured milk	12 measures
Single cream	16 measures
Double cream, whipped	to taste

Non-alcoholic. Sweeten the coffee while hot, then chill. Add the vanilla-flavoured milk and single cream. Chill. Serve in glasses, topped with whipped cream. Serves 4.

7 BRANDY CRUSTA

Sugar syrup	5 ml (1 tsp)
Lemon juice	1 measure
Angostura bitters	1 dash
Maraschino	5 ml (1 tsp)
Orange bitters	1 dash
Brandy	2 measures

Use the shaker. Place a spiral of orange rind in a frosted (crusta) glass, add ice and strained cocktail. Decorate with seasonal fruit.

Clockwise from left: Grapefruit Drink, White Rose Cocktail, Chocolate Cocktail (2), Sherry Sangaree, Tuxedo Cocktail, Iced Coffee, Brandy Crusta (centre).

KÜMMEL

1 SUNSET COOLER

Campari	3 measures
Orange juice	6 measures

Pour into a tumbler, fill up with ice and stir. Decorate with a slice of orange.

2 GIN CRUSTA

Sugar syrup	5 ml (1 tsp)
Lemon juice	1 measure
Angostura bitters	1 dash
Orange bitters	1 dash
Dry gin	2 measures
Maraschino *or* pineapple syrup	5 ml (1 tsp)

Use the shaker. Place a spiral of orange rind in a frosted (crusta) glass, add ice and strained cocktail.

3 DIPLOMAT COCKTAIL

Maraschino	1 dash
French vermouth	2 measures
Italian vermouth	1 measure

Use the mixing glass. Serve with a cherry and a little lemon peel juice squeezed on top.

4 GREEN DRAGON COCKTAIL

Peach bitters	8 dashes
Lemon juice	1½ measures
Kummel	1½ measures
Crème de menthe	3 measures
Dry gin	6 measures

Use the shaker. Serves 4.

5 SILVER STREAK COCKTAIL

Kummel	1½ measures
Dry gin	1½ measures

Use the shaker.

6 EGG PUNCH

Egg	1
Vanilla syrup	15 ml (1 tbsp)
Milk	to taste
Soda water	to taste
Ice	

Non-alcoholic. Beat the egg in a basin, and add vanilla syrup and chopped ice. Use the shaker, then strain into a long glass. Add the milk to three-quarters-fill the glass, then fill up with soda water.

7 HOCK CUP

Hock, chilled	1 bottle
Soda water, chilled	600 ml (1 pint)
Kummel	1½ measures
Brandy	3 measures
Yellow Chartreuse	2 measures
Maraschino	1½ measures

Place a large piece of ice in a glass jug. Add the ingredients, stir well and decorate with fruit. Serve immediately. Serves 4.

From left: Sunset Cooler, Gin Crusta, Diplomat Cocktail, Green Dragon Cocktail, Silver Streak Cocktail, Egg Punch, Hock Cup.

VODKA

1 **WESTERN ROSE COCKTAIL**

Lemon juice	1 dash
Apricot brandy	15 ml (1 tbsp)
French vermouth	15 ml (1 tbsp)
Dry gin	1½ measures

Use the shaker.

2 **INCA COCKTAIL**

Orgeat syrup	1 dash
Orange bitters	1 dash
Dry gin	15 ml (1 tbsp)
Dry sherry	15 ml (1 tbsp)
French vermouth	15 ml (1 tbsp)
Italian vermouth	15 ml (1 tbsp)

Use the mixing glass. Decorate with a slice of orange.

3 **KIR ROYALE**

| Crème de cassis | 2 dashes |
| Chilled champagne | to taste |

Serve in a champagne glass. Stir carefully.

4 **BRANDY COBBLER**

Sugar syrup	5 ml (1 tsp)
Brown curaçao	5 ml (1 tsp)
Brandy	6 measures

Shake or mix well, and strain into a tumbler half-filled with broken ice. Decorate with a slice of orange or lemon and a sprig of mint. Serve with a straw.

5 **SALTY DOG**

| Vodka | 3 measures |
| Grapefruit juice | 6 measures |

Pour the ingredients into an ice-filled, salt-frosted glass and stir. To frost the glass, moisten edges with lemon juice then dip into salt.

6 **CLUB COCKTAIL**

Angostura bitters	1 or 2 dashes
Grenadine	3 dashes
Canadian club whisky	3 measures

Use the mixing glass. Serve with a cherry and a little lemon peel juice squeezed on top.

7 **PORTO FRAISE**

| Port | 3 measures |
| Fraisette | 1 measure |

Mix and serve in the same glass, add water or soda water and a lump of ice. Stir and serve.

Clockwise from bottom left: Western Rose Cocktail, Inca Cocktail, Kir Royale, Brandy Cobbler, Salty Dog, Club Cocktail, Porto Fraise.

AMER PICON

1 WHISKY SOUR

Sugar syrup	5 ml (1 tsp)
Lemon juice	from ½ lemon
Scotch whisky	3 measures

Mix in a shaker, half-filled with broken ice. Strain into a small wine glass. If desired, add a little soda water, and decorate with a slice of lemon.

2 BROOKLYN COCKTAIL

Amer Picon	1 dash
Maraschino	1 dash
French (or dry Martini) vermouth	1 measure
Canadian club whisky	2 measures

Use the mixing glass. Serve with a cherry.

3 PEGU CLUB COCKTAIL

Angostura bitters	1 dash
Orange bitters	1 dash
Lime juice	3 dashes
Cointreau	1 measure
Dry gin	2 measures

Use the mixing glass. Serve with a piece of orange.

4 OPPENHEIM COCKTAIL

Grenadine	15 ml (1 tbsp)
Italian vermouth	15 ml (1 tbsp)
Scotch whisky	1½ measures

Use the mixing glass.

5 SILVER FIZZ

Sugar syrup	5 ml (1 tsp)
Egg white	1
Dry gin	4½ measures
Lemon juice	from 1 lemon
or lemon and lime juice	from ½ lemon and ½ lime

Use a shaker, strain into a highball glass, add ice. Top with soda water, stir. Serve with straws and slices of lemon and/or lime.

6 PICON COCKTAIL

Italian vermouth	1½ measures
Amer Picon	1½ measures

Use the mixing glass. Decorate with a slice of orange.

7 GRAPEFRUIT COCKTAIL (2)

Grapefruit	½
Orange	1
Slices of banana	to taste
Lemon juice	from 1 lemon
Sherry or white wine	15 ml (1 tbsp)

Peel the grapefruit and orange, and break into sections. Arrange round side of a sherbet glass. Add slices of banana. Sprinkle with icing sugar, squeeze over the lemon juice and pour over the sherry or wine.

From left: Whisky Sour, Brooklyn Cocktail, Pegu Club Cocktail, Oppenheim Cocktail, Silver Fizz, Picon Cocktail, Grapefruit Cocktail (2).

BENEDICTINE

1 STRAITS SLING

Lemon juice	from ½ lemon
Angostura bitters	2 dashes
Orange bitters	2 dashes
Cherry brandy	15 ml (1 tbsp)
Benedictine	15 ml (1 tbsp)
Dry gin	3 measures

Use the shaker. Strain into an ice-filled tumbler. Fill up with soda water, and stir. Serve with a cherry and slices of orange and lemon.

2 CARDINALE COCKTAIL

Dry gin	1½ measures
French vermouth	15 ml (1 tbsp)
Campari	15 ml (1 tbsp)

Shake and strain into a cocktail glass.

3 WHISKY RICKEY

Lime juice	from ½ lime
Scotch whisky	4½ measures

Mix in a tumbler with a lump of ice. Fill up with soda water, and stir well. Serve with a slice of lime.

4 ORIENTAL COCKTAIL

Lime juice	from ½ lime
Cointreau	15 ml (1 tbsp)
Italian vermouth	15 ml (1 tbsp)
Canadian club whisky	1½ measures

Use the shaker.

5 CREOLE COCKTAIL

Amer Picon	2 dashes
Benedictine	2 dashes
Italian vermouth	1½ measures
Canadian club whisky	1½ measures

Use the mixing glass. Serve with a little lemon peel juice squeezed on top.

6 FIOUPE COCKTAIL

Benedictine	5 ml (1 tsp)
Italian vermouth	1½ measures
Brandy	1½ measures

Use the mixing glass. Serve with a cherry and a little lemon peel juice squeezed on top.

7 'OH, HENRY!' COCKTAIL

Ginger ale	1 measure
Benedictine	1 measure
Scotch whisky	1 measure

Use the mixing glass.

From left: Straits Sling, Cardinale Cocktail, Whisky Rickey, Oriental Cocktail, Creole Cocktail, Fioupe Cocktail, 'Oh, Henry!' Cocktail.

SLOE GIN

1 PLANTER'S COCKTAIL

Sugar syrup	15 ml (1 tbsp)
White rum	1½ measures
Lemon or lime juice	15 ml (1 tbsp)

Use the mixing glass. Serve with a slice of lime

2 BLACKTHORN COCKTAIL

Orange bitters	2 dashes
Italian vermouth	1 measure
French vermouth	1 measure
Sloe gin	1 measure

Use the mixing glass. Serve with a cherry and a little lemon peel juice squeezed on top.

3 ONE EXCITING NIGHT

Orange juice	1 dash
French vermouth	1 measure
Italian vermouth	1 measure
Plymouth gin	1 measure

Use the shaker. Serve with a little lemon peel juice squeezed on top.

4 CALVADOS RICKEY

Lime juice	from ½ lime
Calvados	4½ measures

Mix in a tumbler with a lump of ice. Fill up with soda water and stir well.

5 BURGUNDY CUP

Brandy	3 measures
Maraschino	3 measures
Benedictine	2 or 3 dashes
Brown curaçao	1½ measures
Burgundy, preferably chilled	1 bottle
Soda water, preferably chilled	100 ml (4 fl oz)

Place a large piece of ice in a glass jug or bowl. Add the ingredients, stir well, decorate with fruit. Serves 4.

6 OPENING COCKTAIL

Grenadine	15 ml (1 tbsp)
Italian vermouth	15 ml (1 tbsp)
Canadian club whisky	1½ measures

Use the mixing glass.

7 SLOE GIN COCKTAIL

French vermouth	15 ml (1 tbsp)
Italian vermouth	15 ml (1 tbsp)
Sloe gin	1½ measures

Use the mixing glass.

* SLOE GIN IS A SWEET RED LIQUEUR, MADE BY SOAKING SLOES IN GIN.

From top left: Planter's Cocktail, Blackthorn Cocktail, One Exciting Night, Calvados Rickey, Burgundy Cup, Opening Cocktail, Sloe Gin Cocktail.

FERNET BRANCA

1 BRANDY FLIP

Egg yolk	1
Brandy	3 measures
Sugar or sugar syrup	to taste

Prepare in the shaker, half-filled with broken ice. Shake well, and strain into a wineglass. Serve with grated nutmeg on top.

2 SLOE GIN RICKEY

Lime juice	from ½ lime
Sloe gin	4½ measures

Mix in a tumbler with a lump of ice. Fill up with soda water, stir well, and serve with a slice of lime.

3 KING COLE COCKTAIL

Fernet Branca	1 dash
Sugar syrup	2 dashes
Scotch whisky	3 measures

Use the mixing glass. Decorate with slices of orange and pineapple.

4 MILLIONAIRE COCKTAIL (2)

Grenadine	1 dash
Lime juice	from 1 lime
Apricot brandy	1 measure
Rum	1 measure
Sloe gin	1 measure

Use the shaker. Decorate with a cherry.

5 PORT COBBLER

Sugar syrup	5 dashes
Brandy	1 or 2 dashes
Port	4½ measures

Mix well, then strain into a tumbler half-full of broken ice. Decorate with fruit, and serve with a straw.

6 BLUE COOLER

Lime juice	from ½ lime
White rum	3 measures
Blue curaçao	1½ measures
Pineapple juice	6 measures

Stir ingredients in a tumbler. Add ice. Serve with straws.

7 BERMUDIAN ROSE COCKTAIL

Dry gin	2 measures
Apricot brandy	1 measure
Grenadine	1 measure
Lemon juice	1 measure

Use the shaker. Decorate with a slice of apricot, if available, and a cherry.

From left: Brandy Flip, Sloe Gin Rickey, King Cole Cocktail, Millionaire Cocktail (2), Port Cobbler, Blue Cooler, Bermudian Rose Cocktail.

DRAMBUIE

1　AFTER-SUPPER COCKTAIL

Cointreau	1½ measures
Apricot brandy	1½ measures
Lemon juice	4 dashes

Use the shaker.

2　BOBBY BURN'S COCKTAIL

Benedictine	3 dashes
Italian vermouth	1½ measures
Scotch whisky	1½ measures

Use the mixing glass. Serve with a little lemon peel juice squeezed on top and a cherry.

3　AFTER-DINNER COCKTAIL (1)

Apricot brandy	1½ measures
Cointreau	1½ measures
Lime juice and grated rind	from 1 lime

Use the shaker. Serve with a slice of orange.

4　STARS AND STRIPES 'A POUSSE-CAFÉ'

Crème de cassis, maraschino and green Chartreuse	in equal quantities

Serve in a pousse-café glass, adding ingredients in the stated order to form a layered effect. Pour liqueurs over the back of a spoon, held so that it touches the sides of the glass.

5　JERSEY LILY (A POUSSE-CAFÉ)

Yellow Chartreuse and brandy	in equal quantities

Serve as above.

6　HOT SCOTCH

Lemon juice	from 1 lemon
Sugar lumps	2
Scotch whisky	3 measures

Put ingredients in a glass, fill up with boiling water, stir well.

7　RUSTY NAIL

Drambuie	1 measure
Scotch whisky	2 measures

Serve in the old-fashioned whisky/rocks way, on ice.

Clockwise from top left: After-supper Cocktail, Bobby Burns Cocktail, After-Dinner Cocktail (1), Stars and Stripes (a pousse-café), Jersey Lily (a pousse-café), Hot Scotch, Rusty Nail.

1 JOHNNIE MACK COCKTAIL

Pernod	3 dashes
Orange curaçao	1 measure
Sloe gin	2 measures

Use the mixing glass. Serve with a little lemon peel juice squeezed on top.

2 PADDY COCKTAIL

Angostura bitters	1 dash
Italian vermouth	1½ measures
Irish whiskey	1½ measures

Use the mixing glass.

3 SHAMROCK COCKTAIL

Green Chartreuse	3 dashes
French vermouth	1½ measures
Crème de menthe	3 dashes
Irish whiskey	1½ measures

Use the mixing glass.

4 DRAMBUIE SWIZZLE

Drambuie	3 measures
Lime cordial	1½ measures
Orange bitters	1 drop
Soda water	to taste

Half fill a tumbler with ice, add the Drambuie, lime cordial and bitters. Top up with soda water, stir. Decorate with a sprig of mint or a slice of lime.

5 PRAIRIE OYSTER

Vinegar	2 dashes
Worcestershire sauce	5 ml (1 tsp)
Tomato ketchup	5 ml (1 tsp)
Egg yolk	1

Non-alcoholic. Mix all the ingredients except the egg yolk. Then drop the egg yolk in the glass without breaking it. Serve with a dash pepper on the top.

6 IRISH COFFEE

Hot coffee	1 serving
Granulated sugar	10 ml (2 tsp)
Irish whiskey	2 measures
Double cream	to taste

Pour coffee into a glass, stir in sugar and whiskey. Pour cream over the back of a warmed spoon, very gently, do not stir.

7 SOUTHERN GIN COCKTAIL

Orange bitters	2 dashes
Cointreau	2 dashes
Dry gin	3 measures

Use the shaker. Serve with a little lemon peel juice squeezed on top.

Clockwise from top: Johnnie Mack Cocktail, Paddy Cocktail, Shamrock Cocktail, Drambuie Swizzle, Prairie Oyster, Irish Coffee, Southern Gin Cocktail (centre).

DARK AND GOLDEN RUM

1 **SENSATION COCKTAIL**

Maraschino	3 dashes
Mint	3 sprigs
Lemon juice	15 ml (1 tbsp)
Dry gin	45 ml (3 tbsp)

Use the shaker. Serve with a cherry and mint, if available.

2 **RUM FIX**

Sugar syrup	5 ml (1 tsp)
Lemon juice	from ½ lemon
Dark or white rum	1½ measures
Cherry brandy	1½ measures
Water	to taste

Place the ingredients in a tumbler, stir. Fill up with crushed ice. Decorate with fruit and serve with straws.

3 **BLUE HAWAIIAN**

White rum	1½ measures
Blue curaçao	15 ml (1 tbsp)
Pineapple juice	3 measures
Coconut cream	1½ measures

Blend with a scoop of crushed ice for a few seconds and serve in a champagne flute with a cherry and a slice of pineapple.

4 **WEST INDIAN COCKTAIL**

Angostura bitters	4 dashes
Lemon juice	3 dashes
Sugar syrup	3 dashes
Dry gin	3 measures

Stir and serve in the same glass, adding a lump of ice.

5 **RASPBERRY COOLER**

Raspberry syrup	1½ measures
Dry gin	1½ measures
Lime juice	15 ml (1 tbsp)
Grenadine	2 dashes
Maraschino	1 dash
Ginger ale	200 ml (⅓ pint)

Place ingredients in a mixing glass. Stir. Pour into a tumbler half-filled with ice.

6 **JAMAICAN COFFEE**

Hot coffee	1 serving
Granulated sugar	10 ml (2 tsp)
Dark rum	2 measures
Double cream	to taste

Pour the coffee into a glass, stir in the sugar and rum. Pour cream over the back of a warmed spoon, very gently. Do not stir.

7 **BITTER COCKTAIL**

Lemon juice	from 1 lemon
Orange juice	from ½ orange
Angostura bitters	3 dashes

Use the shaker, half-filled with broken ice, and strain into a wine glass. A little sugar or sugar syrup may be added, according to taste.

Clockwise from left: Sensation Cocktail, Rum Fix, Blue Hawaiian, West Indian Cocktail, Raspberry Cooler, Jamaican Coffee, Bitter Cocktail.

KAHLUA

1 MILK PUNCH

Brandy	3 measures
Dark rum	1½ measures
Sugar syrup	15 ml (1 tbsp)
Milk	to taste

This may be prepared cold (in the shaker, half-filled with broken ice) or hot (by heating the milk). Serve with grated nutmeg on top.

2 GIN COBBLER

Sugar syrup	5 ml (1 tsp)
Blue curaçao	5 ml (1 tsp)
Dry gin	6 measures

Shake or mix well, and strain into a tumbler half-full of broken ice. Decorate with fruit and serve with a straw.

3 BLACK RUSSIAN

Vodka	1 measure
Kahlua	1 measure

Stir and serve on ice.

4 DRAMBUIE SHRUB

Drambuie	1½ measures
Orange juice, chilled	4½ measures
Lemon water ice	1 scoop

In a goblet, mix the Drambuie and orange juice. Top with water ice. Serve with straws and a small spoon. Decorate with a sprig of mint.

5 WHISKY SMASH

Sugar	½ lump
Mint	4 sprigs
Scotch whisky	3 measures

Dissolve the sugar in water, stir in the mint briefly and remove. Half-fill the shaker with ice, add the whisky, shake and strain. Stir, decorate with fruit and small straws.

6 BRAVE BULL COCKTAIL

Tequila	1 measure
Kahlua	1 measure

Serve over ice in an old-fashioned (whisky/rocks) glass.

7 ATTA BOY COCKTAIL

Grenadine	4 dashes
French vermouth	1 measure
Dry gin	2 measures

Use the shaker. Serve with a little lemon peel juice squeezed on top.

From left: Milk Punch, Gin Cobbler, Black Russian, Drambuie Shrub, Whisky Smash, Brave Bull Cocktail, Atta Boy Cocktail.

FRENCH VERMOUTH

1 PICON GRENADINE

Amer Picon	3 measures
Grenadine	1 measure

Mix and serve this aperitif in the same glass, add water or soda water and a lump of ice. Stir and serve.

2 BLENTON COCKTAIL

Angostura bitters	1 dash
Plymouth gin	2 measures
French (or dry Martini) vermouth	1 measure

Use the shaker. Serve with a cherry and a little lemon peel juice squeezed on top.

3 DAIQUIRI COCKTAIL

White rum	2 measures
Granulated sugar	10 ml (2 tsp)
Lime or lemon juice	15 ml (1 tbsp)

Use the shaker.

4 APRICOT LADY

Golden rum	1½ measures
Apricot brandy	1½ measures
Lime juice	15 ml (1 tbsp)
Orange curaçao	3 dashes
Egg white	2 dashes

Blend with a small scoop of crushed ice for a few seconds. Serve in a large wine glass with a slice of orange.

5 KNICKERBOCKER COCKTAIL

Italian vermouth	1 dash
French vermouth	1 measure
Dry gin	2 measures

Use the mixing glass. Serve with a little lemon peel juice squeezed on top.

6 APPLE PIE COCKTAIL

Apricot brandy	2 dashes
Bacardi rum	1½ measures
Italian vermouth	1½ measures

Use the shaker.

7 WHISKY FIX

Sugar syrup	10 ml (2 tsp)
Lemon juice	from ½ lemon
Scotch whisky	4½ measures
Water	to taste

Place ingredients in a tumbler, stir. Fill up glass with crushed ice. Decorate with fruit and serve with straws.

From left: Picon Grenadine, Blenton Cocktail, Daiquiri Cocktail, Apricot Lady, Knickerbocker Cocktail, Apple Pie Cocktail, Whisky Fix.

GRAND MARNIER

1 ARTIST'S SPECIAL COCKTAIL

Lemon juice	2 measures
Gooseberry syrup	2 measures
Dry sherry	4 measures
Scotch whisky	4 measures

Use the mixing glass. Serve with a slice of lemon. Serves 4

2 ALLIES COCKTAIL

Kummel	2 dashes
French vermouth	1½ measures
Dry gin	1½ measures

Use the shaker.

3 YELLOW DAISY COCKTAIL

Pernod	1 dash
French vermouth	1 measure
Grand Marnier	15 ml (1 tbsp)
Dry gin	1 measure

Use the shaker. Serve with a cherry.

4 TROCADERO COCKTAIL

Orange bitters	1 dash
Grenadine	1 dash
French vermouth	1½ measures
Italian vermouth	1½ measures

Use the mixing glass. Serve with a cherry and a little lemon peel juice squeezed on top.

5 BLUE BOAR

Vodka	45 ml (3 tbsp)
Drambuie	15 ml (1 tbsp)
Blue curaçao	15 ml (1 tbsp)
Lemon squash	1 dash
Egg white	1

Use the shaker. Serve with a flower.

6 ALICE MINE COCKTAIL

Scotch whisky	2 dashes
Italian vermouth	1½ measures
Kummel	1½ measures

Use the mixing glass. Serve with a cherry.

7 ADONIS COCKTAIL

Orange bitters	1 dash
Dry sherry	2 measures
Italian vermouth	1 measure

Use the mixing glass. Serve with a piece of orange.

From left: Artist's Special Cocktail, Allies Cocktail, Yellow Daisy Cocktail, Trocadero Cocktail, Blue Boar, Alice Mine Cocktail, Adonis Cocktail.

AMARETTO DI SARONNO

1 **AMARETTO SOUR**

Lemon juice	1½ measures
Amaretto di Saronno	3 measures

Make in a shaker, half-filled with broken ice. Strain into a frosted tulip champagne glass. Decorate with a slice of orange.

2 **QUIET SUNDAY**

Vodka	3 measures
Amaretto di Saronno	1½ measures
Orange juice	6 measures
Grenadine	1 dash

Mix vodka, Amaretto di Saronno and orange juice in a shaker, half-filled with ice. Strain into an ice-filled tumbler, then add a dash of grenadine.

3 **ORANGE BLOOM COCKTAIL**

Cointreau	15 ml (1 tbsp)
Italian vermouth	15 ml (1 tbsp)
Dry gin	1½ measures

Use the shaker. Serve with a cherry.

4 **BRANDY PUNCH**

Lemon juice	from ½ lemon
Sugar syrup	15 ml (1 tbsp)
Cointreau	2 or 3 dashes
Brandy	4½ measures

Prepare in a shaker, half-filled with broken ice. Strain into an ice-filled tumbler. Decorate with seasonal fruits.

5 **BLUSHING BARMAID**

Amaretto di Saronno	1½ measures
Campari	1½ measures
Egg white	from ½ egg
Bitter lemon	3 measures

Shake Amaretto, Campari and egg white with broken ice. Strain into an ice-filled glass. Top up with bitter lemon, stir. Decorate with lemon, apricot and a cherry.

6 **PORT WINE FLIP**

Egg yolk	1
Port	3 measures
Sugar syrup	to taste

Prepare in a shaker, half-filled with broken ice. Shake well, and strain into a wine glass. Serve with grated nutmeg on top.

7 **SATAN'S WHISKERS COCKTAIL**

Orange bitters	1 dash
Orange juice	15 ml (1 tbsp)
French vermouth	15 ml (1 tbsp)
Italian vermouth	15 ml (1 tbsp)
Grand Marnier	15 ml (1 tbsp)
Dry gin	15 ml (1 tbsp)

Use the shaker. Serve with a slice of orange.

HALLOWEEN BONUS COCKTAIL

Italian vermouth	1 measure
Pernod	2 measures

Use the mixing glass. Serve with a slice of lemon and a cherry.

Clockwise from top: Amaretto Sour, Quiet Sunday Cocktail, Orange Bloom Cocktail, Brandy Punch, Halloween Bonus Cocktail, Blushing Barmaid Cocktail, Port Wine Flip, Satan's Whiskers Cocktail (centre).

BRANDY

1 HOT TEA PUNCH

Freshly brewed tea	1.8 litres (3 pints)
Brandy	600 ml (1 pint)
Dark rum	1 bottle
Sugar	to taste

Mix well, and mull with a red-hot poker. Decorate with orange and lemon peel. Serves at least 12.

2 PORT WINE EGGNOG

Egg	1
Sugar syrup	5 ml (1 tsp)
Port	4½ measures
Brandy	1½ measures
Dark rum	1½ measures
Milk	6 measures

Prepare in a shaker, half-filled with broken ice. Strain, sprinkle with grated nutmeg. Stir in more milk if desired.

3 SCOTCH MILK PUNCH

Scotch whisky	4½ measures
Lemon juice	3 dashes
Sugar syrup	15 ml (1 tbsp)
Milk	to taste

This may be prepared cold (in a shaker, half-filled with broken ice) or hot (by heating the milk). Serve with grated nutmeg on top.

4 DRAMBUIE COFFEE

Hot coffee	1 serving
Granulated sugar	5 ml (1 tsp)
Drambuie	2 measures
Double cream	to taste

Pour coffee into a glass, stir in the sugar and Drambuie. Pour the cream over the back of a warmed spoon, very gently. Do not stir.

5 GLÜHWEIN

Red wine	12 measures
Sugar lumps	2
Lemon	1 slice
Orange	1 slice
Cinnamon	1 pinch

Heat all the ingredients. Serves at least 6.

6 BLACKCURRANT TEA

Blackcurrant jelly	15 ml (1 tbsp)
Sugar lumps	4
Lemon juice	10 ml (2 tsp)

Non-alcoholic. Mix together in a jug, and add a tumblerful of boiling water. Stir well, and stand the jug in a pan of boiling water for 20 minutes. Then strain and serve.

7 OXFORD PUNCH

Dark rum	3 measures
Brandy	2 measures
Lemon squash	1 measure
Boiling water	6 measures
Sugar	to taste

Quantities can be increased to serve any number of persons, provided that the proportions of the ingredients are kept the same. Stir all together in a punch bowl.

Clockwise from left: Hot Tea Punch, Port Wine Eggnog, Scotch Milk Punch, Drambuie Coffee, Glühwein, Blackcurrant Tea, Oxford Punch.

WHITE CRÈME DE MENTHE

1 GOLDEN CADILLAC COCKTAIL

Galliano	1 measure
Single cream	1 measure
White curaçao or Cointreau	1 measure

Use the shaker.

2 BRANDY COLLINS

Sugar syrup	5 ml (1 tsp)
Brandy	4½ measures
Lemon juice	from 1 lemon
or lime juice	from 2 limes

Make in a shaker, half-filled with broken ice. Strain into a tumbler, add ice and fill up with soda water. Stir. Decorate with fruit. Serve with straws.

3 BRANDY HIGHBALL

Brandy	4½ measures
Ginger ale or soda	

Serve in a tumbler with a few lumps of ice. Serve with a piece of lemon peel or a slice of lemon.

4 STINGER

White crème de menthe	15 ml (1 tbsp)
Brandy	45 ml (3 tbsp)

Use the shaker. Serve very cold.

5 MARTINI COCKTAIL (MEDIUM)

Italian vermouth	15 ml (1 tbsp)
Dry gin	1½ measures
French (or dry Martini) vermouth	15 ml (1 tbsp)

Use the mixing glass. Serve with a little lemon peel juice squeezed and then served on top.

6 LORD SUFFOLK COCKTAIL

Maraschino	1½ measures
Cointreau	1½ measures
Italian vermouth	1½ measures
Dry gin	7½ measures

Use the shaker. Serve with a little lemon peel juice squeezed on top. Serves 4.

7 PALL MALL COCKTAIL

Orange bitters	1 dash
White crème de menthe	5 ml (1 tsp)
French vermouth	1 measure
Italian vermouth	1 measure
Dry gin	1 measure

Use the mixing glass.

Clockwise from top left: Golden Cadillac Cocktail, Brandy Collins, Brandy Highball, Stinger, Martini Cocktail (Medium), Lord Suffolk Cocktail, Pall Mall Cocktail.

LILLET

1 NAPOLEON COCKTAIL

Orange curaçao	1 dash
Fernet Branca	1 dash
Dubonnet	1 dash
Dry gin	3 measures

Use the mixing glass. Serve with a cherry and a little lemon peel juice squeezed on top.

2 WHISKY COLLINS

Sugar syrup	5 ml (1 tsp)
Scotch whisky	4½ measures
Lemon juice	from 1 lemon
or lime juice	from 2 limes

Use the shaker, half-filled with broken ice. Strain into a tumbler, add ice and fill up with soda water. Stir. Decorate with fruit. Serve with straws.

3 EMMAGREEN

Dry gin	1½ measures
Orange juice	15 ml (1 tbsp)
Amaretto di Saronno	15 ml (1 tbsp)
Blue curaçao	15 ml (1 tbsp)
Egg white	from ½ egg
Sparkling wine	3 measures
or champagne, chilled	

Half-fill a shaker with broken ice. Shake all ingredients and strain into a frosted tumbler. Top up with champagne.

4 'HOOP-LA!' COCKTAIL

Lemon juice	15 ml (1 tbsp)
Lillet	15 ml (1 tbsp)
Cointreau	15 ml (1 tbsp)
Brandy	15 ml (1 tbsp)

Use the shaker. Serve with a slice of orange.

5 BAMBOO OR REFORM COCKTAIL

Orange bitters	1 dash
Dry sherry	1½ measures
French vermouth	1½ measures

Use the mixing glass. Serve with a little lemon peel juice squeezed on top.

6 'HOOTS MON' COCKTAIL

Lillet	15 ml (1 tbsp)
Italian vermouth	15 ml (1 tbsp)
Scotch whisky	1½ measures

Use the mixing glass.

7 DUBONNET CITRON

Dubonnet	3 measures
Sirop de citron	1 measure

Mix and serve this aperitif in the same glass. Add water or soda water and a lump of ice. Stir and serve. As alternatives to Dubonnet, use Amer Picon, Lillet or Campari.

Clockwise from top left: Napoleon Cocktail, Whisky Collins, Emmagreen, 'Hoop-La!' Cocktail, Bamboo or Reform Cocktail, 'Hoots Mon' Cocktail, Dubonnet Citron.

CRÈME DE CACAO

1 ALEXANDER COCKTAIL (1)

Crème de cacao	15 ml (1 tbsp)
Sweetened single cream	15 ml (1 tbsp)
Dry gin	1½ measures

Use the shaker. Decorate with a chocolate flake.

2 MARTINEZ COCKTAIL

Orange bitters	1 dash
Maraschino	2 dashes
French vermouth	1½ measures
Dry gin	1½ measures

Use the mixing glass. Serve with an olive and a little lemon peel juice squeezed on top.

3 RUM COLLINS

Sugar syrup	5 ml (1 tsp)
Dark or white rum	4½ measures rum
Lemon juice	from 1 lemon
or lime juice	from 2 limes

Make in a shaker, half-filled with broken ice. Strain into a tumbler, add ice and fill up with soda water. Stir. Decorate with fruit. Serve with straws.

4 OLD-FASHIONED COCKTAIL

Sugar lump	1
Angostura bitters	2 dashes
Canadian club whisky	4½ measures
Lemon peel	from ½ lemon

Prepare and serve in a tumbler. Put the sugar in first, then add the Angostura bitters, and muddle. Add the whisky and a cube of ice, and stir. Squeeze lemon peel juice on top.

5 WINTER SUNRISE

Campari	1½ measures
Dry gin	1½ measures
Pineapple juice	6 measures

Pour into a tumbler, fill up with ice, stir. Decorate with fruit.

6 ALEXANDER COCKTAIL (2)

Crème de cacao	1 measure
Sweetened single cream	1 measure
Brandy	1 measure

Use the shaker. Decorate with grated chocolate.

7 ALASKA COCKTAIL

Orange bitters	2 dashes
Yellow Chartreuse	15 ml (1 tbsp)
Dry gin	45 ml (3 tbsp)

Use the shaker. Serve with a little lemon peel juice squeezed on top.

From left: Alexander Cocktail (1), Martinez Cocktail, Rum Collins, Old-fashioned Cocktail, Winter Sunrise, Alexander Cocktail (2), Alaska Cocktail.

TIA MARIA

1 BLUE CRUSTA

Blue curaçao	2 measures
Lemon juice	1 measure
Angostura bitters	1 dash
Brandy	5 ml (1 tsp)

Make in a shaker half-filled with broken ice. Place a spiral of lemon rind in a frosted (crusta) glass. Add ice and strained cocktail. Decorate with fruit.

2 ANGEL'S TIP COCKTAIL

Crème de cacao	2 measures
Single cream	15 ml (1 tbsp)

Float cream on top. Decorate with a little grated chocolate.

3 GRASSHOPPER COCKTAIL

Green crème de menthe	1 measure
White crème de cacao	1 measure
Single cream	1 measure

Shake and serve in champagne glass with straws.

4 NEWTON'S SPECIAL COCKTAIL

Angostura bitters	1 dash
Cointreau	15 ml (1 tbsp)
Brandy	45 ml (3 tbsp)

Use the mixing glass.

5 SPECIAL POUSSE-CAFÉ

Grenadine	5 ml (1 tsp)
Green crème de menthe	1 measure
Galliano	5 ml (1 tsp)
Kummel	1 measure
Brandy	1 measure

Serve in a pousse-café glass, add the ingredients in stated order to create a layered effect. Pour liquids over the back of a spoon.

6 CALYPSO COFFEE

Hot coffee	1 serving
Granulated sugar	5 ml (1 tsp)
Tia Maria	1 measure
White rum	1 measure
Double cream	to taste

Pour the coffee into a wine glass, stir in the sugar, Tia Maria and rum. Pour the cream over the back of a warmed spoon, very gently. Do not stir.

7 SPANISH TOWN COCKTAIL

Cointreau	2 or 3 dashes
White rum	3 measures

Use the shaker.

From left: Blue Crusta, Angel's Tip Cocktail, Grasshopper Cocktail, Newton's Special Cocktail, Special Pousse-café, Calypso Coffee, Spanish Town Cocktail.

1 CROW COCKTAIL

Grenadine	1 dash
Lemon juice	2 measures
Scotch whisky	1 measure

Use the mixing glass.

2 KCB COCKTAIL

Apricot brandy	1 dash
Lemon juice	1 dash
Kirsch	15 ml (1 tbsp)
Dry gin	45 ml (3 tbsp)

Use the shaker. Serve with a little lemon peel juice squeezed on top.

3 GIN HIGHBALL

Dry gin	4½ measures
Angostura bitters	2 dashes
Soda water	

Serve in a tumbler with a few lumps of ice, a piece of lemon peel or a slice of lemon.

4 RUM HIGHBALL

White or dark rum	4½ measures
Lemonade or soda water	to taste

Serve in a tumbler with a few lumps of ice. Serve with a piece of lime peel or a slice of lime.

5 RAFFLES KNOCKOUT COCKTAIL

Kirsch	2 measures
Cointreau	2 measures
Lemon juice	1 dash

Shake, and serve in champagne glass. Add cherries.

6 MARY PICKFORD COCKTAIL

Grenadine	3 dashes
Maraschino	6 dashes
Pineapple juice	1½ measures
Bacardi rum	1½ measures

Use the mixing glass.

7 HOT FRUIT DRINK

Fruit syrup	1 measure
Sugar	to taste
Lemon juice	from 1 lemon

Non-alcoholic. Dilute the fruit syrup with two measures of hot water, add the sugar and lemon juice, and serve.

From left: Crow Cocktail, KCB Cocktail, Gin Highball, Rum Highball, Raffles Knockout Cocktail, Mary Pickford Cocktail, Hot Fruit Drink.

GINGER WINE

1 PORT WINE NEGUS

Port	1 wine-glassful
Lemon	1
Sugar	to taste

Put the wine in a long glass, and add the sugar and the rind and juice of the lemon. Fill up with boiling water, and strain.

2 HEART STIRRER

Amaretto di Saronno	1½ measures
Veuve du Vernay or dry sparkling white wine, chilled	to taste

Pour the Amaretto di Saronno into a champagne glass, then top up with wine. Stir carefully.

3 BUCK'S FIZZ COCKTAIL

Orange juice	from 1 orange
Champagne	to taste

Use a large goblet or champagne glass. Top up the orange juice with champagne.

4 VERMOUTH CASSIS HIGHBALL

French vermouth	4½ measures
Crème de cassis	5 ml (1 tsp)
Soda water or lemonade	to taste

Serve in a tumbler with a few lumps of ice, and cherry, and a piece of lemon peel or a slice of lemon.

5 AFTER-DINNER BLUES

Blue curaçao	1½ measures
Double cream	15 ml (1 tbsp)

Float the cream on top of the curaçao. Do not stir.

6 ORIENT EXPRESS

Drambuie	1 measure
French vermouth	1 measure
Canadian club whisky	1 measure

Use the mixing glass. Stir the ingredients over ice. Strain into a cocktail glass. Serve with a piece of orange peel.

7 THREE MILLER COCKTAIL

Grenadine	3 dashes
Lemon juice	1 dash
Bacardi rum	1 measure
Brandy	2 measures

Use the shaker.

Clockwise from top left: Port Wine Negus, Heart Stirrer, Buck's Fizz Cocktail, Vermouth Cassis Highball, After-dinner Blues, Orient Express, Three Miller Cocktail.

DEMERARA RUM *

1 HOT BUTTERED RUM

Dark rum	30 ml (2 tbsp)
Granulated sugar	10 ml (2 tsp)
Butter	10 ml (2 tsp)
Mixed spice	2.5 ml (½ tsp)

Put the ingredients in a tumbler, fill up with boiling water, and stir well.

2 PRAIRIE HEN COCKTAIL

Vinegar	2 dashes
Worcestershire sauce	5 ml (1 tsp)
Egg	1
Tabasco sauce	2 dashes
Pepper and salt	to taste

Non-alcoholic. Mix all the ingredients except the egg. Then crack the egg into the glass without breaking the yolk.

3 GRAND SLAM COCKTAIL

French vermouth	15 ml (1 tbsp)
Italian vermouth	15 ml (1 tbsp)
Swedish punsch	1½ measures

Use the mixing glass. Serve with a slice of lemon.

4 MONTE CARLO IMPERIAL COCKTAIL

Lemon juice	15 ml (1 tbsp)
Crème de menthe	15 ml (1 tbsp)
Dry gin	1½ measures
Champagne	to taste

Use the shaker. Strain into a wine glass, and fill up with champagne.

5 GRENADIER COCKTAIL

Grenadine	3 dashes
Ginger wine	1½ measures
Brandy	1½ measures

Use the shaker. Serve with a strawberry or a slice of orange.

6 WHISKY SANGAREE

Granulated sugar	5 ml (1 tsp)
Water	3 measures
Scotch whisky	4½ measures

Dissolve the sugar in the water in a whisky tumbler. Add the whisky and fill with crushed ice. Stir well, decorate with grated nutmeg. Serve with straws.

7 ZOMBIE

White rum	1½ measures
Dark rum	1½ measures
Apricot brandy	1½ measures
Orange juice	15 ml (1 tbsp)
Lemon juice	15 ml (1 tbsp)
Pineapple juice	15 ml (1 tbsp)
Demerara rum	1 dash

Use the shaker for all the ingredients except the Demerara rum. Strain and pour into a highball glass half-filled with crushed ice. Pour over the Demerara rum. Garnish with fruit.

* NOTE: DEMERARA RUM IS 151% PROOF.

Clockwise from bottom left: Hot Buttered Rum, Prairie Hen Cocktail, Grand Slam Cocktail, Monte Carlo Imperial Cocktail, Grenadier Cocktail, Christmas Bonus Coffee (add sugar and Benedictine to hot coffee, then pour on double cream over the back of a warm spoon), Whisky Sangaree, Zombie Cocktail (centre).

INGREDIENTS GUIDE

If you have just one or two bottles in your drinks cabinet, this guide will help you to find the cocktails you can make using them. Since most cocktails are based on gin, brandy, rum, vermouth, Scotch whisky, Canadian club whisky or vodka, the cocktails are listed under those headings. To find, for example, a cocktail containing gin and rum, look under the main heading *Gin-based cocktails* and then under the sub-heading *Gin/rum*. The two cocktails you will find listed here do not also appear under *Rum-based cocktails*, avoiding repetition. Mixers and non-alcoholic extras (see page 8 for the list of these) are not included in the ingredients guide.

Gin-based cocktails

Gin only
Belmont Cocktail, 20
Bennett Cocktail, 12
Bulldog Cooler, 10
Café de Paris Cocktail, 32
Clover Club Cocktail, 12
Cream Fizz, 10
Gimlet Cocktail, 10
Gin Daisy, 44
Gin Fix, 58
Gin Highball, 108
Gin Sling, 14
Grapevine Cocktail, 10
Hot Gin, 10
Orange Blossom Cocktail (1), 10
Orange Blossom Cocktail (2), 16
Orange Fizz, 30
Pink Lady Cocktail, 10
Pink Rose Cocktail, 12
Raspberry Cooler, 88
Royal Fizz, 16
Silver Fizz, 76
Strawberry Cream Cooler, 60
Strawberry Dawn, 60
West Indian Cocktail, 88
White Cocktail, 52
Whiz-bang Cooler, 28

Gin/rum
Bacardi Special Cocktail, 42
Roosevelt Cocktail, 54

Gin/vermouth
Atta Boy Cocktail, 90

Bloodhound Cocktail, 60
Cooperstown Cocktail, 46
Knickerbocker Cocktail, 92
Martini Cocktail (dry), 16
Martini Cocktail (medium), 100
Martini Cocktail (sweet), 12
Polo Cocktail, 16
Queen's Cocktail, 16
RAC Cocktail, 16
Velocity Cocktail, 12
Yellow Rattler Cocktail, 16

Gin/vermouth/apricot brandy
Western Rose Cocktail, 74

Gin/vermouth/Calvados
Star Cocktail, 50

Gin/vermouth/Campari
Cardinale Cocktail, 78
Negroni Cocktail, 38

Gin/vermouth/Cointreau
Journalist Cocktail, 26
Luigi Cocktail, 24
Orange Bloom Cocktail, 96

Gin/vermouth/crème de cassis
Parisian Cocktail, 54

Gin/vermouth/Dubonnet
Café Royal Appetiser Cocktail, 14
Dubonnet Cocktail, 14
Royal Cocktail, 14

Gin/vermouth/Grand Marnier
Satan's Whiskers Cocktail, 96

Gin/vermouth/green Chartreuse
Sand Martin Cocktail, 36

Gin/vermouth/kummel
Allies Cocktail, 94

Gin/vermouth/maraschino
Martinez Cocktail, 104

Gin/vermouth/sherry
Inca Cocktail, 74

Gin/apricot brandy
Bermudian Rose Cocktail, 82
Fairy Belle Cocktail, 44
Paradise Cocktail, 44

Gin/apricot brandy/Calvados
Angel Face Cocktail, 50
Prince's Smile Cocktail, 50

Gin/blue curaçao
Blue Bird Cocktail, 40
Gin Cobbler, 90

Gin/Campari
Tropical Dawn, 38
Winter Sunrise, 104

Gin/cherry brandy
Singapore Sling, 46

Gin/cherry brandy/Bénédictine
Straits Sling, 78

Gin/Cointreau
Hawaiian Cocktail, 56
Hula-hula Cocktail, 24
Pegu Club Cocktail, 76
Southern Gin Cocktail, 86

Gin/crème de cassis
Cassis Highball, 56

Gin/crème de menthe
Alexander's Sister Cocktail, 26

Fallen Angel Cocktail, 38
Monte Carlo Imperial Cocktail, 112

Gin/crème de menthe/kummel
Green Dragon Cocktail, 72

Gin/kummel
Silver Streak Cocktail, 72

Gin/maraschino
Gin Crusta, 32
Sensation Cocktail, 88
White Rose Cocktail, 70

Gin/Pernod
Café de Paris Cocktail, 32
London Cocktail, 46
Monkey Gland Cocktail, 24

Gin/Pernod/Calvados
Dempsey Cocktail, 54

Gin/sherry
Roc-a-coe Cocktail, 28

Gin/Swedish punsch
Waldorf Cocktail, 48

Brandy-based cocktails
Brandy only
Brandy Collins, 100
Brandy Daisy, 30
Brandy Flip, 82
Brandy Highball, 100
Brandy Julep, 60
Brandy Smash, 46
Brandy Sour, 26
Cider Cup (1), 22
Grenadier Cocktail, 112
Plain Eggnog, 22

Brandy/white rum
Hot Tea Punch, 98
Oxford Punch, 98
Scorpion, 34
Three Miller Cocktail, 110

Brandy/white rum/port
Port Wine Eggnog, 98

Brandy/vermouth
Charles Cocktail, 22
Washington Cocktail, 22

Brandy/vermouth/Bénédictine
Fioupe Cocktail, 78

Brandy/vermouth/Pernod
Presto Cocktail, 72

Brandy/apricot brandy
Cuban Cocktail, 44

Brandy/blue curaçao
Blue Crusta, 106
Bosom Caresser Cocktail, 40
Breakfast Eggnog, 40
East India Cocktail, 40

Brandy/Calvados
Depth Bomb Cocktail, 68
Depth Charge Cocktail, 58

Brandy/cherry brandy
Brandy Fix, 46
Vanderbilt Cocktail, 46

Brandy/cherry brandy/orange curaçao
Cherry Blossom Cocktail, 62

Brandy/Cointreau
Brandy Punch, 96
Claret Cup, 24
Egg Sour, 24
Newton's Special Cocktail, 106
Rolls-Royce Cocktail, 24
Sidecar Cocktail, 42

Brandy/crème de menthe
Emerald Cooler, 30

Brandy/green Chartreuse
Champs Elysées Cocktail, 30

Brandy/maraschino
Brandy Crusta, 70

Brandy/orange curaçao
Brandy Cobbler, 74

Brandy/port
Port Cobbler, 82
Port Wine Cocktail, 54

Brandy/yellow Chartreuse
Golden Slipper, 68
Jersey Lily (a pousse-café), 84

Brandy/yellow Chartreuse/Pernod
Yellow Parrot Cocktail, 68

Rum-based cocktails
White rum only
Bacardi Cocktail, 38
Casablanca, 34

Cuba Libre, 34
Daiquiri Cocktail, 92
Piña Colada, 34
Plain Eggnog, 22
Planter's Cocktail, 80
Rum Collins, 104
Rum Cooler, 34
Rum Highball, 108

Rum/vermouth/apricot brandy
Apple Pie Cocktail, 82

Rum/vermouth/Blue curaçao
Fair and Warmer Cocktail, 48

Rum/apricot brandy/sloe gin
Millionaire Cocktail (2), 82

Rum/blue curaçao
Blue Cooler, 82
Blue Hawaiian, 88

Rum/brown or orange curaçao
Rum Daisy, 52

Rum/cherry brandy
Rum Fix, 88

Rum/Cointreau
Spanish Town Cocktail, 106
Spring Shake-up, 34

Rum/crème de banane
Banana Bliss, 62
Banana Daiquiri, 62

Rum/Galliano
Barracuda, 62

Rum/maraschino
Mary Pickford Cocktail, 108
Rum Crusta, 34

Rum/Pernod
Bacardi Crusta, 34

Rum/sherry
Quarterdeck Cocktail, 62

Rum/Swedish punsch
Melba Cocktail, 48
Tanglefoot Cocktail, 48

Rum/Swedish punsch/Calvados
Roulette Cocktail, 52
Twelve Miles Out Cocktail, 50

Vermouth-based cocktails

Vermouth only
Addington Cocktail, 28
Club Cooler, 12
Raymond Hitch Cocktail, 12
Trocadero Cocktail, 94
Wyoming Swing Cocktail,

Vermouth/Scotch whisky
Affinity Cocktail, 18
Oppenheim Cocktail, 76
Rob Roy Cocktail, 28
Thistle Cocktail, 18
Wembley Cocktail, 18

*Vermouth/Scotch whisky/
Benedictine*
Bobby Burns Cocktail, 84

*Vermouth/Scotch whisky/cherry
brandy*
Blood and Sand Cocktail, 46

Vermouth/Scotch whisky/kummel
Alice Mine Cocktail, 94

Vermouth/Canadian club whisky
Hot Deck Cocktail, 62
Los Angeles Cocktail, 32
Manhattan Cocktail (dry), 16
Mountain Cocktail, 32

*Vermouth/Canadian club whisky/
Amer Picon*
Creole Cocktail, 78

*Vermouth/Canadian club whisky/
Campari*
Old Pal Cocktail, 42

*Vermouth/Canadian club whisky/
Cointreau*
Oriental Cocktail, 78

*Vermouth/Canadian club whisky/
Drambuie*
Orient Express, 110

*Vermouth/Canadian club whisky/
Dubonnet*
Soul's Kiss Cocktail, 32

*Vermouth/Canadian club whisky/
Swedish punsch*
Boomerang Cocktail, 48

Vermouth/vodka
Vodkatini Cocktail, 36

Vermouth/Amer Picon
Picon Cocktail, 76

Vermouth/crème de cassis
Cassis Highball, 56

*Vermouth/green chartreuse/
Plymouth gin*
Bijou Cocktail, 58

Vermouth/Irish whiskey
Paddy Cocktail, 86

*Vermouth/Irish whiskey/crème de
menthe*
Shamrock Cocktail, 86

Vermouth/maraschino
Diplomat Cocktail, 72

Vermouth/sherry
Bamboo or Reform Cocktail, 102
Greenbriar Cocktail, 48

Vermouth/sloe gin
Blackthorn Cocktail, 80
Sloe Gin Cocktail,

Vermouth/Swedish punsch
Grand Slam Cocktail, 112

Scotch whisky-based cocktails

Scotch whisky only
Crow Cocktail, 108
Gaelic Coffee, 18
Hot Scotch, 84
Scotch Milk Punch, 98
Scotch Mist Cocktail, 18
Whisky Collins, 102
Whisky Cooler, 18
Whisky Daisy, 52
Whisky Fix, 92
Whisky Rickey, 78
Whisky Sangaree, 112
Whisky Smash, 90
Whisky Sour, 76
Whisky Toddy, 18

Scotch whisky/Benedictine
'Oh, Henry!' Cocktail, 78

Scotch whisky/Fernet Branca
King Cole Cocktail, 82

Scotch whisky/Pernod
Linstead Cocktail, 22
Morning Glory Fizz, 26
White Horse Daisy, 20

Scotch whisky/sherry
Artist's Special Cocktail, 94

Canadian club whisky-based cocktails

Canadian club whisky only
Club Cocktail, 74
Commodore Cocktail, 63
Ink Street Cocktail, 42
New York Cocktail, 52
New York Cooler, 32
Old-fashioned Cocktail, 104
Rock and Rye Cocktail, 32
'SG' Cocktail, 58

Canadian club whisky/Blue curaçao
Millionaire Cocktail (1),

*Canadian club whisky/brown or
orange curaçao*
Rye Fizz, 52

*Canadian club whisky/Cointreau/
Dubonnet*
Dandy Cocktail, 36

Canadian club whisky/Pernod
Ladies' Cocktail, 38

Vodka-based cocktails

Vodka only
Bloody Mary, 36
Harvey Wallbanger, 42
Salty Dog, 74
Screwdriver, 36

Vodka/blue curaçao/Drambuie
Blue Boar, 94

Vodka/Campari
SW1 Cocktail, 38

Vodka/Cointreau
Balalaika Cocktail, 36

Vodka/Kahlua
Black Russian, 90

TYPES OF COCKTAIL

Party cocktails
Brandy Punch, 96
Buck's Fizz Cocktail, 110
Champagne Cobbler, 44
Champagne Julep, 58
Cider Cup (1 and 2), 22, 68
Claret Cup, 24
Glühwein, 98
Hock Cup, 72
Hot Tea Punch, 98
Moselle Cobbler, 30
Valentine's Champagne
Cocktail, 22

Long and cool drinks
Angostura Fizz, 14
Apricot Lady, 92
Calvados Highball, 64
Banana Bliss, 62
Banana Daiquiri, 62
Blue Cooler, 82
Brandy Cobbler, 74
Brandy Collins, 100
Brandy Daisy, 30
Brandy Fix, 46
Brandy Highball, 100
Brandy Julep, 60
Brandy Smash, 46
Bulldog Cooler, 10
Casablanca, 34
Cassis Highball, 56
Club Cooler, 12
Cream Fizz, 10
Cuba Libre, 34
Drambuie Swizzle, 86
Emerald Cooler, 30
Gin Cobbler, 90
Gin Daisy, 44
Gin Highball, 108
Gin Sling, 14
Ginger Ale Cup, 50
Grape Cocktail, 56
Morning Glory Fizz, 26
New York Cooler, 32
Orange Fizz, 30

Piña Colada, 34
Port Cobbler, 82
Port Wine Sangaree, 54
Raspberry Cooler, 88
Royal Fizz, 16
Rum Collins, 104
Rum Cooler, 34
Rum Daisy, 51
Rum Fix, 88
Rum Highball, 108
Rye Fizz, 52
Scorpion, 34
Shandy Gaff, 64
Sherry Sangaree, 70
Silver Fizz, 76
Singapore Sling, 46
Sloe Gin Rickey, 82
Spring Shake-up, 34
Straits Sling, 78
Strawberry Cream Cooler,
60
Strawberry Dawn, 60
Sundew Cocktail, 64
Sunset Cooler, 72
True Blue, 40
Vermouth Cassis Highball,
110
Whisky Collins, 102
Whisky Cooler, 18
Whisky Daisy, 52
Whisky Rickey, 78
Whisky Sangaree, 112
Whisky Smash, 90
White Horse Daisy, 20
Whiz-bang Cooler, 20
Wyoming Swing, 24

Non-alcoholic drinks
Blackcurrant Cocktail, 66
Blackcurrant Tea, 98
Bitter Cocktail, 88
Cherry Cocktail, 66
Egg Lemonade, 66
Egg Punch, 72
Ginger Ale Cup, 50

Grapefruit Drink, 70
Grapefruit and Orangeade,
28
Hot Fruit Drink, 108
Iced Chocolate, 66
Iced Coffee, 76
Iced Tea, 56
Mixed Fruit Cocktail, 66
Pineapple Lemonade, 56
Pussy Foot Cocktail, 30
Orangeade, 66
Raspberry Lemonade, 66
Sundew Cocktail, 64

Breakfast cocktails
Bitter Cocktail, 88
Breakfast Eggnog, 40

Special occasion cocktails
Alfonso Cocktail, 14
Barracuda Cocktail, 62
Black Velvet Cocktail, 32
Blue Hawaiian, 88
Buck's Fizz Cocktail, 110
Champagne Cobbler, 44
Champagne Julep, 58
Emmagreen, 102
Golden Dream Cocktail, 42
Heart Stirrer, 110
Kir Royale, 74
Monte Carlo Imperial
Cocktail, 112
Valentine's Champagne
Cocktail, 22

Coffees
Calypso Coffee, 106
Christmas Bonus Coffee,
112
Drambuie Coffee, 98
Gaelic Coffee, 18
Iced Coffee, 76
Irish Coffee, 86
Jamaican Coffee, 88

After-dinner cocktails
After-dinner Blues, 110
After-dinner Cocktail, 84

After-supper Cocktail, 84
Alexander Cocktail (1 and
2), 104, 104
Alexander's Sister Cocktail,
26
Angel's Tip Cocktail, 106
Bobby Burns Cocktail, 84
Chocolate Cocktail (1 and
2), 68, 70
Golden Slipper, 68
Grasshopper Cocktail, 106
Grenadier Cocktail, 112
Jersey Lily à Pousse-Café,
84
Newton's Special Cocktail,
106
Port Wine Cocktail, 54
Raffles Knockout Cocktail,
108
Rusty Nail, 84
Spanish Town Cocktail, 106
Special Pousse-café, 106
Stars and Stripes (a pousse-
café), 84

Dessert cocktails
Drambuie Shrub, 90
Grapefruit Cocktail (1 and
2), 56, 76

Nightcaps
Ale Posset, 28
Hot Buttered Rum, 112
Hot Gin, 10
Hot Scotch, 84
Milk Punch, 90
Plain Eggnog, 22
Port Wine Eggnog, 98
Port Wine Flip, 98
Port Wine Negus, 110
Scotch Milk Punch, 98
Whisky Toddy, 18

Pick-me-ups
Prairie Hen Cocktail, 112
Prairie Oyster, 86

INDEX

A

Addington Cocktail, 28
Adonis Cocktail, 94
Affinity Cocktail, 18
After-dinner Blues, 110
After-dinner Cocktail, 84
After-supper Cocktail, 84
Alaska Cocktail, 104
Ale Posset, 28
Alexander Cocktail (1), 104
Alexander Cocktail (2), 104
Alexander's Sister Cocktail, 26
Alfonso Cocktail, 14
Alice Mine Cocktail, 94
Allen (Special) Cocktail, 68
Allies Cocktail, 94
Amaretto Sour, 96
American Beauty Cocktail, 60
Americano Cocktail, 38
Angel Face Cocktail, 50
Angel's Tip Cocktail, 106
Angostura bitters, 8
Angostura Fizz, 14
anisette, 8
Apple Pie Cocktail, 92
Appetiser Cocktail, 20
Apricot Lady, 92
Artist's Special Cocktail, 94
Atta Boy Cocktail, 90

B

Bacardi Cocktail, 38
Bacardi Crusta, 34
Bacardi Special Cocktail, 42
Balalaika Cocktail, 36
Bamboo or Reform Cocktail, 102
Banana Bliss, 62
Banana Daiquiri, 62
Barracuda, 62
basic equipment, 7
Belmont Cocktail, 20

Bennett Cocktail, 12
Bentley Cocktail, 50
Bermudian Rose Cocktail, 82
Bijou Cocktail, 58
bitter beer, 8
Bitter Cocktail, 88
bitters, 8
Black Russian, 90
Black Velvet Cocktail, 32
Blackcurrant Cocktail, 66
blackcurrant jelly, 8
Blackcurrant Tea, 98
Blackthorn Cocktail, 80
blended cocktails, 9
Blenton Cocktail, 92
Blood and Sand Cocktail, 46
Bloodhound Cocktail, 60
Bloody Mary, 36
Blue Bird Cocktail, 40
Blue Boar, 94
Blue Cooler, 82
Blue Crusta, 106
Blue Hawaiian, 88
Blue Sour, 40
Blushing Barmaid, 96
Bobby Burns Cocktail, 84
Boo Boo's Special, 36
Boomerang Cocktail, 48
Bosom Caresser Cocktail, 40
Brandy Cobbler, 74
Brandy Collins, 100
Brandy Crusta, 70
Brandy Daisy, 30
Brandy Fix, 46
Brandy Flip, 82
Brandy Highball, 100
Brandy Julep, 60
Brandy Punch, 96
Brandy Smash, 46
Brandy Sour, 26
Brave Bull Cocktail, 90
Brazil Cocktail, 28

Breakfast Eggnog, 40
Brooklyn Cocktail, 76
Buck's Fizz Cocktail, 110
Bulldog Cooler, 10
Burgundy Cup, 80

C

Café de Paris Cocktail, 32
Café Royal Appetiser Cocktail, 14
Calvados Cocktail, 54
Calvados Highball, 64
Calvados Rabbit Cocktail, 64
Calvados Rickey, 80
Calvados Sour, 64
Calypso Coffee, 106
Cardinale Cocktail, 78
Casablanca, 34
Cassis Highball, 56
champagne, 8
Champagne Cobbler, 44
Champagne Julep, 58
Champs Elysées Cocktail, 30
Charles Cocktail, 22
Cherry Cocktail, 66
Cherry Blossom Cocktail, 62
Chocolate Cocktail (1), 68
Chocolate Cocktail (2), 70
Christmas Bonus Coffee, 112
Cider, 8
Cider Cocktail, 14
Cider Cup (1), 22
Cider Cup (2), 68
Claret Cup, 24
Claridge Cocktail, 52
Clover Club Cocktail, 12
Club Cocktail, 74
Club Cooler, 12
cocktail sticks, 7
cocktail cabinet, 6
cocktail glasses, 7
cocktail trolley, 6

coconut cream, 8
Commodore Cocktail, 62
Copperstown Cocktail, 46
cream, 8
Cream Fizz, 10
Creole Cocktail, 78
Crow Cocktail, 108
crusta glasses, 7
Cuba Libre, 34
Cuban Cocktail, 44

D

Daiquiri Cocktail, 92
Dandy Cocktail, 36
dashes, 9
decanter bottles, 7
Demararan rum, 112
Dempsey Cocktail, 54
Depth Bomb Cocktail, 68
Depth Charge Cocktail, 58
Diplomat Cocktail, 72
Doctor Cocktail, 48
Drambuie Coffee, 98
Drambuie Shrub, 90
Drambuie Swizzle, 86
Dubonnet Citron, 102
Dubonnet Cocktail, 14
Duchess Cocktail, 20

E

East India Cocktail, 40
Egg Lemonade, 66
Egg Punch, 72
Egg Sour, 24
eggs, 8
electric blender, 7
Emerald Cooler, 30
Emmagreen, 102

F

Fair and Warmer Cocktail, 48
Fairy Belle Cocktail, 44
Fallen Angel Cocktail, 38

Fioupe Cocktail, 78
Fourth Degree Cocktail, 44
Fraisette, 8
fruit, 8
fruit knife, 7

G
Gaelic Coffee, 18
garnishes, 8
Gimlet Cocktail, 10
Gin Cobbler, 90
Gin Crusta, 72
Gin Daisy, 44
Gin Fix, 58
Gin Highball, 108
Gin Sling, 14
ginger ale, 8
Ginger Ale Cup, 50
ginger syrup, 8
ginger wine, 112
Glad Eye Cocktail, 26
Glühwein, 98
Golden Cadillac Cocktail, 100
Golden Dream Cocktail, 42
Golden Slipper, 68
gooseberry syrup, 8
Grand Slam Cocktail, 112
Grape Cocktail, 56
grape juice, 8
Grapevine Cocktail, 10
Grapefruit Cocktail (1), 56
Grapefruit Cocktail (2), 76
Grapefruit Drink, 70
grapefruit juice, 8
Grapefruit and Orangeade, 28
Grasshopper Cocktail, 106
Green Dragon Cocktail, 72
Greenbriar Cocktail, 48
Grenadier Cocktail, 112
grenadine syrup, 8

H
Halloween Bonus Cocktail, 96
Harvey Wallbanger, 42
Hawaiian Cocktail, 56
Heart Stirrer, 110
Hock Cup, 72

'Hoop-la!' Cocktail, 102
'Hoots Mon' Cocktail, 102
Hot Buttered Rum, 112
Hot Deck Cocktail, 62
Hot Fruit Drink, 108
Hot Gin, 10
Hot Scotch, 84
Hot Tea Punch, 98
Hula-hula Cocktail, 24

I
ice, 7, 9
Iced Chocolate, 66
Iced Coffee, 76
Iced Tea, 56
Inca Cocktail, 74
Ink Street Cocktail, 42
Irish Coffee, 86

J
Jack Rose Cocktail, 64
Jamaican Coffee, 88
Jersey Lily (a pousse-café), 84
Johnnie Mack Cocktail, 86
Journalist Cocktail, 26
juices, 8

K
KCB Cocktail, 108
King Cole Cocktail, 82
Kir Cocktail, 54
Kir Royale, 74
Knickerbocker Cocktail, 92

L
Ladies' Cocktail, 38
lemon peel, 9
lemon squash, 8
lemon squeezer, 7
lemon water ice, 8
lime cordial, 8
Linstead Cocktail, 22
liqueurs, 7, 8
London Cocktail, 46
Lord Suffolk Cocktail, 100
Los Angeles Cocktail, 32
Luigi Cocktail, 24

M
Manhattan Cocktail (dry), 42
Margarita, 60
Martinez Cocktail, 104
Martini Cocktail (dry), 16
Martini Cocktail (medium), 100
Martini Cocktail (sweet), 12
Mary Pickford Cocktail, 108
Melba Cocktail, 48
milk, 8
Milk Punch, 90
Millionaire Cocktail (1), 40
Millionaire Cocktail (2), 82
Mississippi Mule, 56
mixed cocktails, 9
Mixed Fruit Cocktail, 66
mixers, 8
mixing glass, 7
mixing spoon, 7
Monkey Gland Cocktail, 24
Monte Carlo Imperial Cocktail, 112
Morning Glory Fizz, 26
Moselle Cobbler, 30
Mountain Cocktail, 32
muddler, 7

N
Napoleon Cocktail, 102
Negroni Cocktail, 38
New York Cocktail, 52
New York Cooler, 32
Newton's Special Cocktail, 106
Nick's Own Cocktail,
nutmeg grater, 7

O
'Oh, Henry!' Cocktail, 78
Old-fashioned Cocktail, 104
Old Pal Cocktail, 42
olives, 7
Olivette Cocktail, 58
One Exciting Night, 80
Opening Cocktail, 80
Oppenheim Cocktail, 76
orange bitters, 8

Orange Bloom Cocktail, 96
Orange Blossom Cocktail (1), 10
Orange Blossom Cocktail (2), 16
Orange Fizz, 30
orange juice, 8
Orangeade, 66
Oranges and Lemons Cocktail, 26
orgeat syrup, 8
Orient Express, 110
Oriental Cocktail, 78
Oxford Punch, 98

P
Paddy Cocktail, 86
Pall Mall Cocktail, 100
Paradise Cocktail, 44
Parisian Cocktail, 54
peach bitters, 8
Pegu Club Cocktail, 76
petites flutes, 7
Piccadilly Cocktail, 44
pickled onion, 8
Picon Cocktail, 76
Piña Colada, 34
pineapple juice, 8
Pineapple Lemonade, 56
Pink Gin Cocktail, 58
Pink Lady Cocktail, 10
Pink Rose Cocktail, 12
Plain Eggnog, 22
Planter's Cocktail, 80
Polo Cocktail, 16
Port Cobbler, 82
Port Wine Cocktail, 54
Port Wine Eggnog, 98
Port Wine Flip, 96
Port Wine Negus, 110
Port Wine Sangaree, 54
Porto Fraise, 74
Prairie Hen Cocktail, 112
Prairie Oyster, 86
Presto Cocktail, 72
Prince's Smile Cocktail, 50
Pussy Foot Cocktail, 30

Q

Quarter Deck Cocktail, 62
Queen's Cocktail, 16
Quiet Sunday, 96

R

RAC Cocktail, 16
Raffles Knockout Cocktail, 108
Raspberry Cooler, 88
Raspberry Lemonade, 66
Raymond Hitch Cocktail, 12
Rob Roy Cocktail, 28
Roc-a-coe Cocktail, 28
Rock and Rye Cocktail, 32
Rolls-Royce Cocktail, 24
Roosevelt Cocktail, 54
Roulette Cocktail, 52
Royal Cocktail, 14
Royal Fizz, 16
Rum Collins, 104
Rum Cooler, 34
Rum Crusta, 68
Rum Daisy, 52
Rum Fix, 88
Rum Highball, 108
Rusty Nail, 84
Rye Fizz, 52

S

'SG' Cocktail, 58
SW1 Cocktail, 38
St Germain Cocktail, 30
Salty Dog, 74
Sand Martin Cocktail, 36
Satan's Whiskers Cocktail, 96
Scorpion, 34
Scotch Milk Punch, 98
Scotch Mist Cocktail, 18
Screwdriver, 36
Secrestat bitters, 8
Sensation Cocktail, 88
shaken cocktails, 9
shaker, 7
Shamrock Cocktail, 86
Shandy Gaff, 64
Sherry Sangaree, 70

Sidecar Cocktail, 42
Silver Fizz, 76
Silver Streak Cocktail, 72
Singapore Sling, 46
Sirop de citron, 8
Sloe Gin Cocktail, 80
Sloe Gin Rickey, 82
soda water, 8
Soul's Kiss Cocktail, 32
Southern Gin Cocktail, 86
Spanish Town Cocktail, 106
sparkling drinks, 8, 9
Special Pousse-café, 106
spirits, 8
Spring Shake-up, 34
Star Cocktail, 50
Stars and Stripes (a pousse-café), 84
Stinger, 100
stirred cocktails, 9
strainer, 7
Straits Sling, 78
Strawberry Cream Cooler, 60
Strawberry Dawn, 60
straws, 7
sugar, 8
sugar crystals, 8
Sundew Cocktail, 64
Sunset Cooler, 72
syrups, 8

T

Tanglefoot Cocktail, 48
Tequila Sunrise, 60
Third Degree Cocktail, 26
Third Rail Cocktail, 64
Thistle Cocktail, 18
Three Miller Cocktail, 110
Tiger's Tail Cocktail, 20
Tipperary Cocktail, 50
tomato ketchup, 8
Trocadero Cocktail, 94
Tropical Dawn, 38
True Blue, 40
Tuxedo Cocktail, 70
Twelve Miles Out Cocktail, 50

V

Valentine's Champagne Cocktail, 22
vanilla syrup, 8
Vanderbilt Cocktail, 46
Velocity Cocktail, 12
Vermouth Cassis Highball, 110
Vodkatini Cocktail, 36

W

Waldorf Cocktail, 48
Washington Cocktail, 22
Wembley Cocktail, 18
West Indian Cocktail, 88
Western Rose Cocktail, 74
Whisky Collins, 102
Whisky Cooler, 18
Whisky Daisy, 52
Whisky Fix, 92
Whisky Rickey, 78
Whisky Sangaree, 112
Whisky Smash, 90
Whisky Sour, 76

Whisky Toddy, 18
White Cocktail, 52
White Horse Daisy, 20
White Rose Cocktail, 70
Whiz-bang Cocktail, 20
Whiz-bang Cooler, 28
wine, 8
Winter Sunrise, 104
Worcestershire sauce, 8
Wyoming Swing Cocktail, 24

Y

Yellow Daisy Cocktail, 94
Yellow Parrot Cocktail, 68
Yellow Rattler Cocktail, 16

Z

Zombie, 112